David N

Connecting with the Bliss of Life

Powerful lessons for living a peaceful and happy life

Special First Edition

Let the journey begin...

Connecting with the Bliss of Life

D. Michael Ferruolo, Enterprises
PO Box 6421
Laconia, NH 03246
(603) 556-4360
(603) 556-4361 fax
www.daveferruolo.com

ISBN: 0-9767424-9-7

Printed in the United States of America

www.daveferruolo.com

Explore your potential to live the amazing
adventure life is meant to be.

Contents

For my Mother
Whose zest for living life to its fullest and seeking out
fun and enjoyment is a rare and sought after quality in
today's chaotic world.

For my Father
Whose dedication to his profession and commitment to
forge his own destiny gained him the respect of family,
friends and community.

From the melding of these two worlds, I give
thanks for all that I am and all that I am capable of.

For my Son
May you carry forth and achieve what I can only
imagine. The world is your infinite playground—
enjoy it.

Foreword
by Steven D. Farmer, Ph.D.
Author of *Power Animals* and *Sacred Ceremony*

I first met Dave Ferruolo in a class called "Angel Therapy Practitioner Training™" (ATP) that my wife (Doreen Virtue) was teaching and that I was assisting with. In a class of about 150 people, typically there's anywhere from 10-15 men and the rest women, and that was the case with this one. On the first day I noticed this rather muscular guy with dark hair, dark features, an intense gaze, and a strong presence. He definitely stood out. Here was a man on a mission—a spiritual quest—and one who had the courage and willingness to explore many facets of spirituality, including the angelic realm.

As I got to know David both during and after the class, I learned that he had been on this quest for several years, that the ATP course was another step along the way of gathering his spiritual resources in order to fulfill his destiny. He was enthusiastic and purposeful in his seeking. I hold deep respect for anyone on a spiritual path, and he was most certainly heeding the call. Not only did he possess considerable depth and intelligence, he's someone you would appreciate having by your side in a pinch.

Through our conversations I learned that he had been a Navy SEAL, had extensively studied and practiced martial arts, was an accomplished musician, and on top of that, he was a master scuba diving instructor. These credentials impressed me, but more than that, I knew this man was a natural leader and would most likely eventually become a spiritual teacher himself. I was struck by his willingness to continue evolving and learning, opening himself readily to new experiences—a true spiritual explorer.

Connecting with the Bliss of Life is evidence of Dave's emergence into this role as a spiritual teacher. You'll find his insights valuable, accompanied by stories and examples that demonstrate the usefulness of the spiritual principles he writes about. Through stories of his own personal struggles he traces the development of the spiritual philosophy he writes about, echoing in greater details the great mythologist Joseph Campbell's call to "follow your bliss." More than just an invitation to do whatever feels good, he inspires the reader to review his or her life, to take steps to heed the voice of Spirit and align his or her intent with Spirit's intent.

Dave Ferruolo has done the homework necessary to justify his writings and teachings. He has no pretense of being perfect or having all the answers, but as he has done so remarkably well in his life, he encourages the reader to explore, to not settle for the mundane as a dominant force in his or her life, to be willing to risk change when hearing the call, to live life to its fullest and with as much passion and vitality as possible. He offers suggestions for action steps as well as ways of analyzing and contemplating your past, present, and future life path.

I trust you'll find yourself inspired and motivated as you read this book.

Blessings,
Steven Farmer, Ph.D.

For more information about Steven Farmer, please visit his website at: www.stevendfarmer.com

Note:

All the stories in *Connecting with the Bliss of Life* are true; however, most of the names and some of the situations have been changed to honor the privacy of those who were willing to share their lives with us.

"Nothing is more important than reconnecting with your bliss. Nothing is as rich. Nothing is more real."

- Deepak Chopra

Chapter 1
Realizing Bliss

It is said that to be human is to suffer, and yes this world can be a painful, harsh place. It is the way you look at things that dictates the circumstances surrounding your life and the way you perceive the world. Contentment comes from within, and no amount of searching or material gain will lead you to happiness.

Letting the stress of unplanned or unwanted events influence the way you react to and view the world will always lead to turmoil. Living with a mind-set of negativity and fear will blind you to the miraculous flow of bliss, which is within and around you always.

Every day, I witness people leading chaotic lifestyles, responding like robots to the circumstances of their lives, creating more dissonance and conflict. They seek solace in the next best thing, person or position they can find, but always end up frustrated and wondering why they are not truly happy. It is a conundrum of sorts. Sadly, it is self-perpetuating. Stress, negativity and unpleasant reactions to everyday situations only beget more of the same experiences on a deeper level. This, of course, creates undue stress on your body, mind and spirit. This is not blissful living.

Why is it that so many people only see the negative side of our surroundings and situations, while some look upon life with optimism and zeal? What separates those who live happy, harmonious lives from others who exist in discord?

The lessons in *Connecting with the Bliss of Life* can help lead you to that tranquil, harmonious state we all desire by helping you recognize and move beyond negative and fearful thinking. Learn how to bid farewell to the stress and frustration in your life and recapture that childish joy and enthusiasm you once lived with. The key to change is within you. Know you have the power, through choice and intention, to live a harmonious and joy-filled life. Bliss is nothing more than happiness in its highest form. Isn't that what we all strive for... happiness?

Connecting with the bliss of life is a choice you can make right away. I'm not going to tell you, "Just say 'no' to suffering." We will all experience suffering at some point in our lives. I'm not going to tell you to, "Just take the bad with the good." Life can be better than that. Instead, I'm going to show you how to make it all good, to minimize suffering and easily access bliss. When you have learned to do this, your life will be nothing less than amazing.

The bliss of life surrounds us every moment of every day. Bliss is not something that needs to be attained through deed, service or achievement. You do not have to work to attain a state of bliss in your life. It has nothing to do with whether you feel deserving of happiness or if blissful living is something you are worthy of. You may not be perfect, but as a human being, you are the most treasured thing in the world. Because you exist, without doing anything at all, you deserve bliss. You deserve bliss because of nothing you have done or not done, nor because of who you think you are or are not. You deserve it because you are alive. Blissfulness is free for the taking for all those who consciously and deliberately choose it.

I spent the better part of twenty years frustrated and unhappy with my life. Although I accomplished much more than I could ever have imagined possible, I still lived in a state of dissatisfaction. One would think being a Navy SEAL (the elite special warfare unit) would have been the pinnacle of my life, but I looked upon my military profession with disdain. Then I was living my childhood dream, playing guitar in a rock band, but irritability and aggravation permeated the mood of that environment. Years later, while running my scuba diving company, a day job that many people envied, I felt only petulance and exasperation. I dated many great women from all walks of life, but all my relationships ended in disaster. I moved from state to state, career to career and woman to woman, with no psychological or emotional liberation. I felt lost and I was suffering. I was wasting this precious life and something had to change. And one day, it did.

I often hiked to help temporarily alleviate the stress in my life. Being in the mountains took me to another place where I could, if only for a short time, escape the turmoil of my life. Waking up one morning angrier and more stressed than usual, I decided to forego work and hike a mountain near my home. As I stomped my way to the top, each footstep reverberated with anger. Hiking always helped relieve my anxiety, but I was finding little release this day. I knew I could not go on living like this. I had to figure something out, and fast. For almost a decade, I was unhappy and frustrated with wherever I was and with whatever I was doing. I knew my own choices had brought me to where I was, but that only made me feel worse. I had made the choices, so I must have deserved to feel that way. Despite my best efforts, I was not where I thought I would be. My business was extremely time-consuming and stressful, money always seemed short, my relationships were disastrous and I felt utterly alone in the world.

When I reached the summit, I found a quiet place to sit and think. I looked out and took in the beauty of the mountains and lakes. The warm summer breeze felt good on my face, and the many sounds of nature slightly quieted my mind and eased my tension. Exhausted, I laid back on a huge boulder to relax. I felt helpless and I prayed for an answer to come my way. My head was pounding so I closed my eyes and quickly fell asleep. I woke about forty minutes later, feeling kind of strange. As I refocused my vision out over the breathtaking landscape, everything seemed surreal. It was so quiet, peaceful and unaffected by the chaotic state of the world. It was as if my worries and frustration were still sleeping. For a moment I thought perhaps I was just dreaming, but I was not. I wondered why life could not be this peaceful all the time. I took a deep breath and felt myself expanding into the vastness of the mountains. For the moment, I was on top of the world. Anything seemed feasible, and my mind was open to all the amazing possibilities of what I could do and be. I was elated—in a pure state of momentary ecstasy. If only it could last.

As I sat relishing the moment, I had what some might call an epiphany. I realized that all my problems were still waiting for me at the bottom of this mountain. Nothing had changed, yet something seemed very different. Why was I so happy here and now on the top of this mountain, but not happy at the bottom?

I sat thinking about this for a while, and then something occurred to me. I had heard it many times before, but never really grasped the concept. Bliss is a state of mind—a choice, a simple choice. While in sleeping meditation on the mountain, I had unconsciously connected with the flowing bliss of life. What if I actively chose to stay in this state as I hiked down the trail? Would it work, could it work? I decided to try. I figured if I could mentally bring myself back to this spot whenever I began to feel stressed or overwhelmed, I could reconnect with that feeling of bliss.

Before I left the serene summit for the turbid waters of normal life, I captured the essence of the moment in my head. I took a mental snapshot of the scenery, the smells, the sounds, and how I felt at that moment in time—empty of stress, full of peace. What I did next was the key to my success; in my mind, I created a Bliss Box—a special gold box for that moment to exist. In it, I put the embodiment of everything that helped to create the perfect peace I felt. I tied up the box with a gold ribbon and placed it on a storage shelf in my mind. I knew I could count on opening it later, and in the days that followed I was thoroughly amazed to find how well my Bliss Box worked.

A few days later, I got a call on my cell phone from an employee who worked at my scuba diving shop. I was immediately annoyed. Employees were only supposed to dial my cell phone in an emergency. "Sorry to call you, but, um, I have a problem," he said. I became even more irritated. I could hear a man in the background yelling and swearing. My employee continued, "I've got this guy here who says he's going to hurt me if I don't give him a new scuba tank. I did a visual inspection of his tank and it failed." We only fail diving tanks if there is a serious safety issue that could endanger customers and employees. These tanks are filled with 3000psi. That's over a million foot-pounds of kinetic energy. If a tank ruptures, people will die. We don't take chances when it comes to safety.

As I listened, the man proceeded to push my employee onto the floor and demanded reimbursement for his failed cylinder. I hollered for my employee to call 911, and then my cell phone failed. I was helpless. I was worried about my employee and about the store. The entire situation made me very angry and my blood was starting to boil. I felt my old SEAL mentality creeping up, and I knew that was extremely dangerous for everyone involved. As a former member of the elite military anti-terrorism unit and a black belt in several martial arts, I was more than able to deal with this problem.

I closed my eyes, took a deep breath and reached for my Bliss Box. As I exhaled, I mentally untied the ribbon and removed the lid. I saw the mountains, smelled the pine and the rock moss, and heard the wind and the birds. I tried to remember how I felt there, to recall the peacefulness, the bliss. It worked. I instantly began to feel calmer. With that calmness, my thoughts became clearer. Instead of throwing my phone, running angrily to my truck and speeding to the store as I once would have, I calmly but quickly walked to a place where my phone worked, and called 911. When I finally arrived at the dive shop, the police were there and my employee and store were fine. We both gave our accounts to the police officer who responded, and let the law handle the situation from there.

In the days that followed, I was thoroughly amazed to find that my Bliss Box experiment worked over and over again. When I felt myself becoming irritable and flustered, I closed my eyes, took a deep breath and opened my Bliss Box. As I exhaled, I felt peacefulness within me. I finished that week the happiest I had been in many years. I began to touch on the secret of being blissful all the time. Knowing I could choose my state of mind changed everything. I quickly realized that, with practice, I could make my choice a habit. From that day forth, I became a "bliss technician." That is, I wanted to know and master all I could about living a more peaceful life.

Connecting with bliss took lots of time, learning and practice. It still takes daily active thought—but I am no longer a slave to stress and frustration. I realized that most of my problems were caused by my own negative thinking patterns and destructive habits, which were brought on by my perceptions of how life should be. Now, I have developed the habit of choosing positive thoughts and constructive reactions to the situations around me. I wake up every day and intend to be happy. I am only human, and far from perfect. Choosing bliss is often a battle I lose, but I try to learn the lessons from the situations of my life and to be just a bit better than I was yesterday. I live life to the fullest and to the best of my ability. Now life is truly a grand adventure every day.

Know that you deserve bliss and allow yourself to move beyond negative and destructive habits. They have never served you. Make the choice to connect with bliss and live life as it should be... Amazing.

Bliss Technician Process:
Building the Bliss Box

1. Find a place, either in a daydream or in reality, where you feel completely content. This can also be a memory of a time when you were very happy.
2. In your mind, create a special box fro this place or memory to live. Choose its size, texture and color.
3. Put your blissful thoughts into your box. Make sure you include all of the senses. What do you see, smell, hear, taste, and feel (physically and emotionally)?
4. Carefully close your newly created bliss box, and put it in a special place in your mind. Visualize an alter, a special room or a shelf that is easy to access by thought.
5. When you feel any stress, anger, or frustration, you will follow these steps. Even when your stress subsides and you begin to feel peaceful, continue through the following process. Remember the goal is not simply survival, but bliss.

1. Close your eyes and think of your bliss box, and how beautiful it is.
2. Gently touch your bliss box, and feel its warmth. Feel the peacefulness which comes from inside.
3. Take the bliss box and hold it close to your heart. Feel your stress subside, as warmth and harmony from within the box encompasses you.
4. Open your bliss box, and breath in the essence of the sacred place inside. Allow stress to dissipate—let it go, as you view the magical place inside.
5. Mentally seat yourself inside your bliss box. All your worries are now gone, as a shell of peace, serenity and love encapsulates you. As you open your eyes, you are connected with the bliss of life.

"Worry does not empty tomorrow of its sorrows,
it empties today of its strength."

- Corrie Ten Boom

Chapter 2
The Turmoil of Everyday Life

Every one of us, on a daily basis, is bombarded with situations that can create turmoil and stress in our lives. Many of these events are unplanned and unanticipated. We sometimes have no control over what crosses our path, but we do have a choice about how we react to these testing situations. Being defensive and responding to situations with fear, self-protection and force only elevates and empowers the negativity of every person involved. This builds up inside of you and is carried with you all day, fueling more negativity and stress as you deal with people and situations throughout the day. No wonder so many people are frustrated and unhappy.

It does not matter if you are an accountant, a taxi driver, a lawyer or janitor, a movie star or a chef. Stress is a hunter and we are its prey. We are open targets, ready to absorb all the negativity, rudeness, anger, violence, bitterness and sadness of the world. We take all in, amplify it and turn it back to society with a vengeance. It's an awful, sad state. We don't even realize how much it engulfs our way of life. All we know is that life has stopped being fun, and there is little reward for all our efforts. Escalating over the years, stress builds and takes its place in our minds as "the way it is." We accept this state of mind as natural and normal. We accept these habits and behaviors for others and ourselves. Our spirits cry out in rebellion, but we are deaf to its constant pleading. Yet we can never fully squelch that voice in our heads that says things can be better than this. We all long for peace and happiness. This creates yet another conflict in the raging battlefield of our minds.

The battle between your ego mind and your spiritual higher self is the toughest bout of them all. You can always hide from the world, distance yourself from others and take some time away from the daily rituals of your life, but the ego and spirit are with you always. It's the battle of right and wrong, serenity versus discord, love versus hate, passion versus numbness, inner peace versus outer turmoil.

When stress becomes overbearing, it can trigger the "fight or flight" response. If you are aggressive by nature, stress may manifest as anger, rage, violence, hostility or belligerence. A passive person may react by being timid, quiet, or retreating, or feeling shame, nervousness or fearfulness.

These situations are all too common in today's world. If you take an objective look at the situations occurring all around you on a daily basis, you will begin to see the senselessness of it all. Take a few situations, for example, that I have recently witnessed. Peoples' reactions to rather minor irritations in daily life are quite funny sometimes. However, the humor is quickly diminished when we see the pain that stress brings into peoples' lives.

Example 1. Rita is getting ready for work. She rushes around, trying to beat the hands of time on the wall clock. As she opens the front door to leave, her dog runs out into the fenced-in yard. She reacts in a sudden verbal outrage, yelling at the dog to get her butt in the house. The little dog meekly walks back into the house. Rita then slams the door violently and drops her keys, provoking another profane outburst—directed at the dog. She gets to work three minutes late. When her first client arrives, she conveys her dramatic story of how the dog made her late.

Example 2. I'm in line at the bank on a rather slow day. A man comes in with a huge tin can of coins. He goes directly to the front of the line and puts the can on the counter. The woman in front of me starts fidgeting, tapping her foot on the ground and constantly looking at her watch. She keeps looking at the man, then to the back of the line. When the next teller is available, the woman lets out a loud sigh and a stomp of her foot. She peers at her watch, whispering something under her breath. She doesn't even realize the man has moved over and the teller is calling her to the counter. When the woman finally notices—as everyone else has—she lets out an "oh..." and proceeds to the counter. When the woman is finished, she storms out of the bank, making a slight scene, as she pushes her way past a few people coming in to do business.

Example 3. A friend of mine has what she calls a "near-death experience" as she drives home from work. She approaches an intersection with a turn lane and a straight lane. The traffic is light, moving at about 35 mph. She is in the lane heading straight, towards downtown. The light turns yellow and she speeds up a bit to make it through before it changes. A car in the left turn lane suddenly speeds up, with its blinker on, nudging in front of her vehicle. The elderly man in the other car holds his hand out the window waving, as his little car with out-of-state plates overtakes her. My friend slows a bit, hauls on the horn and yells, "You stupid jerk! That's a turn lane!" She tells me how inconsiderate elderly drivers are and how she thinks they all should have their licenses revoked. I ask her why she was speeding through a yellow light. She calls me a jerk and says I don't understand.

In each of these cases, it is the person's perception of the situation that causes them stress. Rita created a stressful situation in her mind by requiring herself to be at work at a certain time, no matter what, even if she had no clients. The woman at the bank created stress for herself as well. She might have had a job interview or a doctor's appointment, or a plane to catch. However, in any of those cases, her stress would have been due to her own poor planning and not the man who had a prearranged appointment to cash in his coins. My friend at the traffic light also created her own stress. By rushing through a yellow light, it was she— not the lost old man—who was actually the antagonist of the story.

When you see the world through implacable eyes, brought on by the illusions of stress, you live a constantly defensive life. You are always justifying the attacks upon youself and reacting in un-loving, violent and rude ways. You see every situation as a personal attack and you have to constantly defend yourself from all these worldly opponents. As you analyze the above situations, you can probably see the humor of each of them. As you think about it, you'll recognize that each of the reactions of these individuals was unnecessary. A calm mind can see the senselessness of it all, but when the mind is clouded with stress, mounting frustration and frenzy within can result in negative and destructive behaviors, which may hurt all involved.

This is a senseless way to go through life. The road to change is easier than you may think. If you can simply change the way you view the world, the world you see will change. If you fill your mind with thoughts of beauty, forgiveness, thankfulness, harmony and love, then the chaotic life you lead will transform wonderfully into harmonious, blissful living.

Bliss Technician Process:
Identifying Stress

Start a journal to keep track of your progress. In this journal, create a stress log. In this log, you will identify the situations in which you became stressed and/or irritated. A few times a week, review your stress log and think about how you could have reacted more peacefully to benefit everyone involved. Ponder each situation for several moments and really think if the stressful reactions we warranted or necessary. Could the situation been avoided or changed for the better by acting out of a place of love and not hate or fear?

"Where there is charity and wisdom, there is neither fear
nor ignorance. Where there is patience and humility,
there is neither anger nor vexation. Where there is
poverty and joy, there is neither greed nor avarice.
Where there is peace and meditation, there is
neither anxiety nor doubt."

- Saint Francis of Assisi

Chapter 3
A Blissful Life

Bliss has many meanings throughout the world,
but sometimes it's quite ambiguous. I have found many
people do not understand what bliss actually is. They
often try to externalize the meaning. Bliss is not a
possession, or something you have to earn. It cannot
truly be understood or conceptualized. We cannot
mathematically or scientifically dissect it into parts and
analyze the components. However, there are many
things we do know about the meaning of bliss.

Bliss is a state of peace, happiness and
contentment. It is a state of mind that anyone can attain
by choice, a state of mind in which we choose to be
happy, joyful and harmonious with others, the world
and ourselves.

It is amazing what can happen in your life when
you choose to rid your mind of negative, destructive
thinking and adopt thoughts of love and peace. When
you stop trying to control the circumstances and
outcomes of your life, and just see where life brings you.
When you decide live in the present, and not dwell in
the past or be fearful of the future... when you realize
your life is perfect as it should be, and when you finally

become aware, your mind will suddenly be freed of the destructive habits that are wasting precious moments of your life. Stress will begin to lift from your mind and a serene harmony will settle in your soul. When you submit to the philosophy that there just may be a better way, you will begin to connect with the natural flow of bliss, and your life will become miraculous.

This perfection of life is how things were meant to be—no matter what your social status, occupation or situation. It is amazing to watch the synchronicities of life unfold before your eyes, catapulting you effortlessly through each blissful day. When you live in a state of everlasting bliss, doors continually open, and you'll find opportunity everywhere. People are always offering unsolicited help and lending a hand, positive situations unfold readily before your eyes. Don't be in awe or think you're just having a lucky day. Know that bliss, which radiates from your soul, is a super magnet for all you need and desire in your life. The more you connect with the bliss of life, the more opportunity and miracles will come your way.

When your mind is calm and blissful and not focused on the bombardment of every-day negativities, your intuitive self will awaken. Your instincts will become keener as you begin to recognize and gain a better understanding of your inner needs and deepest desires. Trust your gut feelings. They will guide and lead you to amazing situations and people.

Beware, though. As you begin to allow your intuition to guide your actions, your normal daily routine will be a thing of the past. New spontaneity will overcome you. You will have sudden compulsions to visit new places. You will be interested in subjects never before on your mind. Strangers will suddenly seem intriguing, as you will be magnetically drawn to talk with them. New friends will appear, bringing fun, joy and excitement to your life. Doors will open before you, presenting many interesting and amazing opportunities.

Recently, on vacation in California, I had the opportunity to befriend a gentleman from England named Michael. Michael is a talented musician, who truly lives a blissful life, allowing and trusting his intuition to guide him. Because Michael has opened his mind to the bliss of life, opportunities and good fortune find him everywhere. Over breakfast one day in Laguna Beach, Michael recounted the tremendous opportunities presented to him while he was in California.

One afternoon, Michael and his travel companion were looking at jewelry from a specialty designer. Michael and the designer got talking and she invited him to participate in a music circle in Malibu. Some Hollywood actors and musicians were going to be socializing there. Michael was excited to participate and meet some of America's Hollywood heroes. As Michael's new friendship with the designer grew, another great opportunity was presented to him. He was asked to be a teacher and guest at a spiritual retreat in Hawaii. "What awesome news!" I thought.

A few months later, Michael emailed to say that he had been invited to travel to India, Bombay and Cochin. Michael told me he would be flying to Kona, Hawaii for the holidays, and then embarking on an incredible adventure to Bangkok for a stay in a palace as a guest of a Balinese princess.

Michael is a prime example of a person completely connected with the bliss of life. He is a testimony to the amazing things that can happen when you go through life with peace and in harmony.

Connecting with bliss can dramatically change the circumstances of even the most negative situation. There is a sunny side to every rainy day. When you connect with the bliss of life, you will realize rain is necessary, and above the clouds the sun is shining. You will be led to wonderful situations, bringing you a more fulfilling life and attracting many people who understand and support you for who you are and what you believe in.

After twelve years in business, I was faced with a grave situation, which jeopardized my career and family. I was operating out of the same location for nine years and was well established. The building itself was not up to my standards, and I grew frustrated with the daily routines of housekeeping. The place was infested with spiders and mice, the roof leaked and there was a buried fuel tank in the basement, which emitted a nasty oily smell every time it rained. The building had virtually no insulation and the foundation had a large hole in it. This made heating in the winter an enormous expense and cooling in the summer next to impossible. Over the years, the landlord continually raised the rent while shirking his responsibility for maintenance. It took him three years to patch the leaks in the roof. The old pane-glass windows were only replaced when they were falling off the building. The illegal fuel tank and the holes in the foundation were never considered. I grew tired of the condition of the building and the constant rent increases, but I had been warned by another business owner never to confront the landlord.

I decided to negotiate a better lease for my business. I would sign a long-term lease if the price was reasonable and repairs were made. Six months before my lease was up, I requested a copy of the new lease. I received no reply. Several months later, I saw my landlord at the post office and he asked bluntly if I was staying or leaving. I told him I requested a copy of the new lease months ago, but he said he never got the message.

Spring was in the air, and I was very busy running the business. I had forgotten about the lease. One day, an employee of the landlord came to my shop with a lease. He placed it in front of me and said I had to sign it right then. I politely said I would look it over first. Again, it had a rent increase with no improvements.

I had a meeting with the landlord to talk about my occupancy. To my surprise, the landlord told me that if I didn't like the lease, to move out. He said if I didn't like the building, to fix it myself; he would do nothing. He gave me one week to sign the lease or he was kicking me out. Instead of seeing me as the secure, long-term tenant I was, he would not compromise. He was willing to see my business move. I could not understand this logic, and thought perhaps it was a business tactic to get me to agree to the new lease.

I let a few days go by and sent in a revised lease, which seemed more than fair for both parties. Again, he told me no and that if I did not sign the lease immediately, he would evict me.

I knew I had lost the battle, and I was fuming over my inability to control the situation. I was caught between a rock and a hard place, and I had no choice but to sign the lease and do the necessary repairs myself. I went back to my office and signed the lease he had given me, and when I had a free moment I would walk it over to him. A few days passed and my landlord, along with one of his employees, came to my shop. He had an aggressive, bitter look on his face. As he came through the door, I greeted him by saying "You win, here's the signed lease." What happened next stunned me, and my working employees. I was met with viciousness. I was told in an outburst of profane abuse that he no longer was going to rent to me and I was to vacate immediately. I told him I had the lease right here, but he said he didn't care and I was to leave immediately; he was going to start the eviction process that day. The nastiness of the situation amazed me. It propelled me into a defensive, vengeful mind-set. I was consumed by stress, anger and fear and, for several weeks, was crippled with the fear of losing my business, my income, my home and my ability to take care of my son.

After contacting a lawyer to file suit and mounting my retaliatory attack, I took off to spend time in the wilderness. I spent two days hiking and meditating in the New Hampshire forests. I held my Bliss Box closely and re-established a peaceful mind-set. I calmly thought over the situation, and suddenly everything became clear.

For many years, I was dissatisfied with my business situation. Although it was profitable, I did not feel fulfilled. I knew there was something bigger and better out there for me. The responsibilities of my business kept me enslaved and unable to pursue my true heart's desire. My creativity and ambitions were shelved, while I struggled to maintain my composure in a frustrating situation.

I began to realize that closing my business was a blessing in disguise. As my mind fell silent I was in a spiritual bliss. I detached myself from the negativity of the situation. I changed my judgments of the landlord to thoughts of thankfulness and forgiveness. I called off my lawyer, and I instantly found a place to move my shop. The new location offered everything I needed to keep my income and allow me the extra time to pursue my dream of writing books and speaking for a living.

Soon after the move was complete, I began my writing career. On a trip to California, I met some fantastic people who catapulted my book ideas into reality. Their help and support enabled me to focus and to complete several works in a short time. They taught me the "ins and outs" of the business and directed me to others who could greatly help my writing career. Change was very scary for me, and the path ahead was different and completely unknown. I trusted that my instincts would accurately guide me. I did not know where I was going, but I was happier than I had been in many years. Connected with the bliss of life, I accepted my unknown future with childish enthusiasm. My path from that day since has been so amazing, I feel as if I'm living a dream.

There are many people, blissfully living magnificent, fulfilling lives. These people effortlessly glide through life, seemingly untouched by the negativity, abuse and harshness of the world. These enlightened souls always have a cheerful, welcoming smile, even in the face of adversity, pain, loss and suffering. People connected with the bliss of life always seem to come out on top, no matter how bad a situation may seem. It appears that they have been touched by the silver spoon of life, gracefully living in the good and avoiding the unpleasant.

So how does one attain this ecstatic, blissful state of peace and harmony? Impossible as it may seem, it is a gratifying and rewarding process for those truly willing to make the journey.

After you realize your level of negative and pessimistic thinking, you must be dedicated to make the change and set a crystal clear intention to do so. You must truly, above all else, want the change to occur. You have to realize that the bliss of life surrounds you and is already within you. It is only a matter of perception. You can only see what you focus your attention on. If you focus on the negativity in your life, you will find it everywhere you look. But if you choose to only see how peaceful life is, you will find peace.

Negativity and all pessimistic and unconstructive thoughts must be eradicated from your mind. You must post mental sentries to intercept all these hurtful thoughts and transmute them into positive, loving energy. As your mind clears and quiets down into a more blissful state, you will begin to see the true beauty in all that exists. You will see through the masks of fear and protection, as the true blissful soul in everyone and everything becomes clear. Realize now that the material, outside world, does not define you. You are yourself, in all your power, grace, beauty and peacefulness. Your ability to forgive and love will be great, bringing peace and harmony into your life.

Friends and strangers alike will seek your council because you radiate light and have the ability to lovingly speak the truth. You will be admired and scorned, but mere words will be the same to you, because to be blissful means to walk the path without judgment of yourself or others.

Bliss Technician Process:

In your journal, write how your life would change if you could attain bliss anytime you wanted. Pen a short story of how your future will be as you begin to connect with the bliss of life every day.

Next, in the "stress" section of your journal, take a look at each stressful occasion you've written about. Then, re-write each occurrence as if when it happened, you dealt with the stress immediately, and you found your path to bliss. Remember to write exactly what you did to find bliss in each situation. Continue by writing how your peaceful resolve to each situation affected others involved and how their day may have been better by your positive actions.

"If half-a-century of living has taught me anything at all,
it has taught me that nothing can bring you peace
but yourself."

- Dale Carnegie

Chapter 4
What's Keeping You?

You know the saying "You are your own worst enemy?" Well, that may be true in many cases. You are the only thing standing in your way of living a truly blissful life. You are your only excuse for not changing or not wanting to change. You are your sole source of procrastination. You are the owner of your time and space. You and you alone choose how you live each and every moment. We all fall into the "I'll do it sometime" trap. The trick is to catch yourself when you enter into projects or tasks that steer you clear of what is truly important in your life. We are all co-creators of our destinies. We choose our course in life with every breath and with every step we take. Take control, with intent, focus and discipline, and your life will surely be amazing.

Connecting with the bliss of life is free. We only have to put forth the effort to change how we focus our thoughts and how we view the world. We were meant to live in peace and harmony, but somehow, somewhere along the way we lost the connection. The wires in our heads got crossed, and we started to see all the evil and hate of the world instead of the beauty and love. When we finally stop following the need to fulfill urges of ego and clear our thoughts of negativity, we can reconnect with the bliss of life and center ourselves in our true natures.

The most important tool we all have is the ability to make a decision and follow it. When I finally realized I had a choice whether to he happy and blissful or live in disharmony, I chose bliss. And it is a choice you can make too. Like any other new process, you will have to practice and train yourself to notice when you are in a stressful state. You then have to exercise your ability to make decisions and take actions that will bring you closer to your goals. You can choose to be in a good mood or you can let the physiological stress response rule your emotions and mind-set. There is a mind-body connection and, with practice, you can control and direct your state of being to happiness and bliss, rather than stress and fear.

It's like changing the channel on the TV when you do not like what you see. If something you do not like comes on the television, you simply change to a different station. Without thought, you just automatically pick up the remote and switch to a different show. Our minds have scripts, which continually run, both in our conscious and sub-conscious minds. Rather than changing the movie in our heads, we have grown accustomed to letting those scripts control our lives. We have learned over the course of our lives to react to certain things in certain ways. We form mind-sets and emotional habits, which we fall prey to and allow them to guide our decisions and way of life. We must realize we are in control of our thoughts and we have the ability to re-write the scripts of our lives. Simply put: choose to be happy, and you will be.

We cannot control other people and situations, but we do have control over our reactions and mind-sets. We can choose to replace the old scripts that no longer serve us. We can re-write the mind's movie to be more harmonious and blissful in any situation.

One of my scripts is the waiting in line mind-script. Many of us do not like waiting in lines, whether it's at the bank, grocery store or ticket counter. I know in the past I have found myself getting very antsy and stressed whenever I was forced to be herded like cattle to my destination. I would look at my watch, tap my foot, cross my arms and stare at my final objective. I would whisper under my breath things like, "Come on!" and "What the hell is taking so long?" Sometimes, I would get so worked up I would just storm out and come back at a later time.

This, of course, never accomplished anything positive. I did not get what I needed and I was stressed for the rest of the day. Besides, I had to go back later and take more time to get what I wanted. As I was able to recognize the self-generated script that controlled my reaction to waiting in a line, I was able to circumvent and change my response to the entire situation. I found out that if I focused on changing my physical reactions and body posture, my mental state would change as well. Instead of the defensive postures of crossed arms, angry foot tapping, and the under-the-breath rude comments, I tried to just relax, smile and think of positive things. The process is easy. When I find myself getting nervous in a line, I close my eyes and take a deep breath. I then relax my shoulders, slowly open my eyes and deliberately put a smile on my face.

It is amazing how well this simple technique works. I often take it a step further, by filling my mind with happy, blissful thoughts, and telling myself I am in a peaceful, serene state. It does not matter if there is a line or not. Why should I let that small thing upset my inner peace? I shouldn't. And neither should you. Choose to be happy and blissful, in all situations, every moment of every day. Make peace and happiness your number one priority and goal every day and in every situation.

You have the power to make the choice. No situation is beyond your ability to control your inner harmony and bliss. One of the most powerful examples of controlling your emotions and state of mind in adversity is a story of Paramahansa Yogananda, the famous Hindu Yogi who brought his teaching to America in the 1920s.

The story goes, while walking at night in an east coast city, several muggers accosted Yogananda and his traveling companions with knives. The muggers aggressively demanded money. In the face of impending danger, Yogananda kept his calm and inner peace.

The story continues that he softly and calmly pulled out his wallet and extended his hand out to the assailants. He stared into their eyes and peacefully said, "Is it money you want? Then, here, take it." Apparently miffed by Yogananda's inner strength and exuding peacefulness, the muggers put their weapons away, apologized and ran off, not taking goods from anyone in the group. Paramahansa Yogananda's choice was to keep his cool in a very dangerous situation. If he had reacted with fear, the outcome may have been very different.

Ultimately, as you continually write the scripts in your mind to play ones of peace, joy and harmony, and you persistently choose to live in a state of bliss, it will become your normal way of life. You will find in a very short time your reactions to unpleasant, uncontrollable situations will be much less stressful, and you will begin having a good day, every day. Unpleasant situations will always arise, but with your choice not to react with stress, anger and fear, you will quickly find a place of peace and lasting bliss. As you lead, others will follow.

People have the habit of social referencing in stressful situations. When people do not know how to act, they look over to the next person and adopt their reaction. One person reacting negatively to a situation can affect everyone involved. Even those who may be having a good day can be affected by someone else's level of stress.

I was about eight years old the first time I went to a baseball game with my father. I was extremely excited. It was at Fenway Park, and the Red Sox were playing their rivals, the Yankees. I didn't know about any of that age-old rivalry stuff. I was just thrilled to watch the plays, to be in a huge crowd of cheering people, and to eat those Fenway Franks. I was very happy until my father began to boo. I missed what he was booing at, so the next time, I watched carefully. I learned that I should boo every time the guys in the pinstriped uniforms made a good play or got a hit. The better those players did, the more stressed and angry my father became, and his actions affected me and caused me stress. After a few games, I did not like going anymore.

If your demeanor is one of calmness and peace, others will strive to emulate your behavior. You will soon find the people in your life moving toward a more harmonious existence, following your lead. Through your actions and quiet dedication to living with bliss, you will set an amazing example for others to follow. Your actions will have the domino effect; stress and dissonance will soon topple and give way to a much quieter, simple way of living.

With your choice to eradicate stressful, aggressive reactions from your behavior patterns, and replace the scripts of your mind with love, peace, excitement and vigor, you will send a rippling wave of bliss, which will affect all those around you. What a beautiful world this would be if we could all live in peace and harmony. As John Lennon would say, "Imagine."

Bliss Technician Process:

In your journal, list the reasons why you're not living in a constant state of bliss. What is wrong in your life? List specific examples. For each example, state how your life would change if you were to confront each of these problem areas with a different mind-set—if you were able to look at each issue from a state of bliss.

Continue to examine your problem areas, and identify what state of mind your non-blissful reactions came from. What were you afraid of? Why did you get so angry? What is the root of your insecurity?

Ask yourself if these fears are warranted. Where did they come from? Do they serve you in any positive way? What is keeping you from abolishing these negative mind-set and bad habits from your life? Write all your thoughts in your journal, no matter how painful the process may be.

Remember that energy in equals energy out. The more thought and effort you put into these processes, the stronger the result. You will heal quicker and be able to move forward to a more blissful life

"What lies behind us and what lies before us are small matters compared to what lies within us."

- Ralph Waldo Emerson

Chapter 5
Making the connection

Most of us would love to live a happier, more blissful life. So why don't we? Again, it is those old worn out patterns of negative thinking and programmed responses that have been passed down to us and taught to us by family, teachers, society and the media. We are trained to be frustrated and angry when things do not go right. We were shown how to worry by our parents and grandparents. We were conditioned by our friends, co-workers and family members to be hostile when things go wrong. Everywhere we look, we find more affirmations that stress and negativity are normal. Our society has adopted this dissonant and unforgiving way of life as the normal routine. We happily accept it as normal, as we complain our lives away. I find it sad to see what people do to their friends, co-workers and family. I find it even more disturbing that most put up with it and accept it readily.

Loral works as an office manager, and has been with the company for almost ten years now. Although the job pays well and offers great insurance for her family, she continually complains of her boss's rude demeanor. He constantly talks badly about the employees, is very condescending and seems to not care about their feelings and the fact they all are doing a great job for him. He offers only criticism, while these people dedicate their lives to helping him.

Loral has actually hung up on me as we talked on the phone, for fear of getting yelled at for being on a personal call—even though she was on a break. This has been going on for years, and every time I ask her why she continues to allow him to treat her and the other employees that way, her answer is always the same. "It's just the way he is. You get used to it. I just tune him out and ignore him when he is in one of his moods." From what I have seen, she must need to wear earmuffs daily, because he is always in one of his moods. When I ask why she doesn't go to another office, she replies; "Why? It's the same everywhere. They're all that way."

Loral's co-workers have also accepted and enabled their boss to be the way he is. They have trained him to stay a jerk as well as he has trained them to indulge his moods. It seems totally acceptable for all of them. Furthermore, in response to his aggressions, some employees get frustrated and retaliate by silently making things difficult for their boss and sometimes even for the customers.

It seems that without the drama we have created for ourselves, life gets boring. You can stop the process. As mentioned in chapter 4, "What's Keeping You?" you can choose to connect with the positive, blissful energy of the universe. You can choose your reactions to others' behaviors. A smile is contagious and so is a good mood. If someone is having a bad day and taking it out on you, simply smile and go about your day. Their poor attitude should not affect your day, should it? If you spread love and joy to everyone you meet, the energy will carry.

At the grocery store last week, I noticed a very jovial cashier. She said hello to everyone who came to her aisle and she wore a huge smile. She asked everyone if they had found everything okay and if she could do anything else for them. She talked about the good weather and the coming of spring. Her great, blissful attitude affected all the people who were in her line. People perked up, smiled and talked back, then walked out of the store appearing much happier than when they had come in. Folks in others aisles looked over to get a glimpse of the happy teller. They, too, seemed mesmerized by her joy. A simple smile goes a long way and can change the mind-set of people dramatically.

So, how do we make the change? We first have to identify the areas where we need improvement. Sometimes it is easier to think backwards than forward, so think of the person you would like to be. Think of yourself, as if you were living a harmonious, blissful life. If you were connected to the flowing bliss of the universe, how would you act and react to the current situations in your life? If you only acted out of love and compassion and with forgiveness, what would it be like? How would it feel if you were smiling and happy all the time? Even in the face of adversity, when confronted with aggression and anger, you would stay calm and in a good mood. Imagine what it would be like.

Next, look at yourself as you are now. How close to your ideal are you? Be truthful, because the more you really understand about your current habits, the easier the change will be. You have to also ask yourself if you really want to change. Do you want to live a blissful life or do you want to wallow in the muddy pond of dissonance? Connecting with the bliss of life is a choice and you have the power and ability to make it happen. It takes a little work.

Once you set your intention to be more blissful in your life, you will find that things start going more smoothly almost immediately. When you wake up every morning and affirm: "Today, I choose to live with joy and harmony. I will be forgiving and compassionate. I will send loving thoughts to everyone I come in contact with. I choose to connect with the bliss of life. Today, I will choose to live happily," your life will magically transform before your eyes.

You have to know that this may not be an easy task at first, but, with practice, you will easily find yourself living joyfully. You must be focused and catch yourself when you are falling into old routines. You will settle back into the old habits occasionally, but with determination and effort, you will keep your thoughts afloat above the negative, destructive patterns you once lived by.

It is very important not to stress yourself if you are unable to connect with bliss at first. Like any new process, it takes time, patience and practice. Occasionally, you will fall back into your old habits and routines. These are the times to catch yourself and consciously direct your thoughts back to the bliss of life. You mustn't be hard on yourself, and it is very important to laugh. Give yourself a pat on the back when this happens, and know you are well on your way to mastering your thoughts. Remember to be peaceful and happy, and when situations bring out the old habits and negativity, just smile.

It is your choice whether to make the connection with bliss or not. The techniques are simple, if you are willing to try. You must learn to get out of your own way and know that all your reasons for not connecting with the bliss of life and living a peaceful, harmonious life are your own self-generated illusionary walls. Trust yourself more and know that joyous living is only a decision away.

Bliss Technician Processes:

Carry your journal with you. As you start to employ the methods for achieving bliss, catch yourself. When you choose a blissful state over stress, congratulate yourself. Write about these moments so that when you fail to connect with the bliss of life, you can go back and prove to yourself that you are capable.

Connecting with the bliss of life is a choice you will have to continually make until it becomes a habit—second nature. Do not get discouraged when you react out of fear. Everyday you will have the chance to choose bliss over stress. Just move forward and learn from the experience, and know you are a better person for even trying.

"Never allow your day to become so cluttered that you neglect your most important goal—to do the best you can, enjoy this day, and rest satisfied with what you have accomplished."

- Og Mandino

Chapter 6
Clean Up Your Life

Being blissful does not mean ignoring or becoming unaware of the circumstances and situation around you. It means being more in touch with yourself and active in your decisions when you respond to your surroundings. To walk the path of bliss is to adopt an attitude of taking care of the little things, which need to be done as they arise. It also means knowing when not to do something when your plate is already full. Your list of things to do will never be complete, so concentrate on the things at hand that you can have an effect on. Pick and choose the activities that either need to be done or are healthy for your spiritual, emotional and psychological growth. Do not dwell on another day's tasks when there is much to focus on today. This will only cause you stress. It is counter-productive to cram too many activities into your life.

It is important to know where you are at every moment and not have your energy and thoughts scattered about in all directions. You have to master the ability to focus on the tasks and time at hand. Planning for future endeavors is very wise, but don't allow it to consume your thoughts. Many people waste too much time thinking and talking about hypothetical happenings or chores and neglect what needs to be done now. I often hear people say, "I'll get to it later". I personally have spent many days worrying and thinking about what I might have to do and always seem to forget what I should be doing. Then, when today is over, I become stressed because I accomplished nothing, and tomorrow's schedule is already full. I have also filled my days with many activities that thwart my efforts for harmonious living. Much power and bliss comes from taking command of the simpler things in life. It is also wise to look at your busy schedule to see what you can cut out. Sometimes even good things have to be sacrificed to get into a more creative and productive flow.

After ending a long-term relationship, I filled my days with as many possible events and plans as I could. It seemed to make the weeks go by faster—to be immersed in schedules and tasks. I dedicated myself to going to the gym for several hours a day, three to four times a week. I also scheduled hikes, diving, movies and dinner activities with friends. At the time, I had my son three to five days a week and was working full time.

Engrossing myself in non-stop activities helped pass the time, but soon I began to feel stressed and I had problems fitting all those good things into my schedule. Everything had become rushed and haphazardly done. My work was suffering, as I spent too much time doing other things. As the home and work projects grew, I knew I had to cut back and simplify my life. What would I cut out of the schedule? I was not doing anything counterproductive—the activities I was doing were all good for mind and body. I had to evaluate what was important and prioritize my daily schedule better. After weighing heavily the pros and cons of my routine, I knew I had to cut the fifteen hours a week I was spending at the gym—for a while anyway.

After I committed to that decision and followed through, I was so much happier and relaxed. Instead of rushing around all day trying to keep up with my schedule, I was able to finish all my business tasks and personal chores with plenty of time left over for a few hikes and dinners with friends. At work, I was much more relaxed, creative and innovative, which spurred higher business productivity and profits. Finally, I found the time to take care of the looming yard work and home chores that had piled up over the months. Once these things were done, I felt so much freer and happier. I had to cut out one of the things I loved in order to reach that state, but it was well worth it.

As I simplified my life and schedule, I found the time to finish the many things that had been going undone and causing stress in my life. I found that when I finally cleaned and organized my home and tended the yard, I became more harmonious and able to concentrate better. There is something about waking to a clean, orderly home that enables me to start the day happy and peaceful.

When your personal spaces are clean, you will be happier and more accommodating during the workday. Conversely, when home chores have built up, the stress carries over into the rest of the week. A clean home promotes productivity. Freedom is the feeling of control over your environment, where you live, what you own and your personal workspace.

If our spaces are disorderly, it will take energy away from the things we need to do. When our homes, cars and offices are cluttered, we unconsciously segment a portion of our minds to continually thinking about cleaning and organizing. Clutter is very frustrating and can cause stress when we incessantly focus on it. Just seeing life in disarray puts us in a mental state of irritation. The annoying stuff chaotically strung around our lives sucks up a lot of energy and keeps us in a constant state of mental debt. We get frustrated with the mess we are in charge of, and the cycle continues by becoming overwhelming when we think of all the other duties we are committed to during our day. Our minds can never be free to relax when we are continually taxed with a cluttered life.

I have adopted a Zen-like mind-frame when it comes to cleaning and organizing my home and workspace. Zen, in this case, can be defined as constant and continual actions for the progression and realization of goals without actively thinking about it. It becomes a habit that involves taking action without really thinking. It's not necessarily a task on your list, but habitual actions that you perform, without even thinking about them, as you go about your day. Keeping a clean life is not something you can schedule in on Sundays, between brunch and the football game; it is a constant, ongoing habit that must be done always. Healthy people don't obsess over their homes, but if they walk by a glass that has been left out, they will bring it to the sink right at that moment. Train yourself to notice these things. If you are on you way to the garage, check to see if the trash needs to be taken out. If the chairs at the kitchen table are skewed, right them as you walk through the dining room. Cleanliness should become a mind-set, a sub-script that runs constantly in the depth of your subconscious. Like the spell-check option in computer programs that instantly points out mistakes, a cleanliness mind-set can instantly alert you to something that's dirty or out of place. If you make it a point to automatically and constantly be in a cleaning and organizing mind-frame, you will always have a neat, orderly home—and you won't have to wait until Sunday to get it done. When the dust starts building up and things become disorganized, it takes a lot of time and hard work to get it back in order. It is much easier to take care of it as it happens than to schedule it in at a later date.

Both my grandfathers were masters of the Zen mind-set when it came to yard work and car maintenance. Papa Mike was a master of the garden and Grandpa Jim was the master of his car. Papa Mike, or "Gramps," as the family called him, would not walk across the grass or by the garden without pulling a weed or plucking a long blade of grass. He would walk his property several times a day, tending to the small, seemingly insignificant matters of grass and garden. Of course, the property always looked perfect. Neighbors and passersby were always envious. Gramps could not visit a yard, in summer or winter, and not pluck a weed or kick some snow from the walkway.

Likewise, Grandpa Jim could not walk past his car without picking a bug off the grill or wiping a water spot off the hood. His car, bought in 1965, still looked and smelled like new when he passed away in 1990. I remember when I was a child; he would check the tire pressures and fluid levels several times a week. He would clean his vehicle of trash at the end of every day. It received a thorough washing inside, outside and underneath every week, all year round. Papa Jim's green Mustang was twenty-five years old and never broke down or needed major service.

Both my grandfathers have since passed away, but I will always remember the perfection of their yard and car. The yard Papa Mike once kept up by himself has never seen such beauty and perfection again. The lawn of the new owners, despite their crew of professional landscapers, cannot compete with the constant efforts of this one special man.

My grandmother has gone through three cars in the past fifteen years, as opposed to the one car in the twenty-five years when her husband, Jim, was alive.

We can learn powerful lessons from these two wise teachers. Through their constant actions of maintenance, they produced not only a beautiful landscape and safe transportation, but also a blissful mental haven within which they could relax and enjoy themselves. I will never forget the smile of satisfaction on Papa Mike's face as he looked out over the yard he kept. As he sat for dinner, he would often say to me, "I can relax and eat now. Today's work is done."

The cleanest space in my house is the bathroom. Although I keep a fairly neat and clean home, my bathroom is always immaculate and sanitary. I clean my bathroom every day. It only takes a few minutes. I keep some cleaner and paper towels on the shelf and every time I use the facility, I wipe a portion of the room down. I may quickly wipe out the sink and clean the mirror one time and the toilet and tops of the washer and dryer the next. When asked what room in my home is my favorite, I always say the downstairs bathroom. My second favorite room is the spare bedroom. Again, it is always neat and organized. I also have an affinity for my back yard and tend to spend some time every day making it look good.

Zen-mindedness is not about killing yourself with a huge list of tasks you must complete, but it is about calmly and actively spending small amounts of time, all the time, in keeping chores at bay. If we strive to constantly do a little bit all the time, then we will never have to do a lot at once.

As soon as you have adopted this philosophy, you will always have a clean, neat living area. You will have to train yourself at first to actively pursue cleanliness and organization. Once you finally do, your home will always be a blissful sanctuary for you to relax in and enjoy.

Creating a blissful home environment is an extraordinary base to work from, but we also need to extend this sanctuary beyond the home. We can easily transform our offices or workspaces the same way we renovate our homes. The habits of clean-mindedness can follow us everywhere we go, including the workplace. We can easily change and manage the energy of the spaces we have control over, but we can never change or control the actions of others.

Friends can be wonderful allies on the road to cleanliness and bliss but unfortunately, some can be detrimental and stifling. It is important to realize you have a choice about the people you spend time with. There are so many more unknown and potential friends in the world who will be more than happy to join you on the path to bliss. There is no reason to allow yourself to be dragged down by the negativity and bad habits of current acquaintances.

For example, if you are trying to lose weight, yet every time you go to lunch with the folks from the office, they order fried foods and desserts, choose not to accompany them anymore. If the break room is filled with smokers and you are trying to quit, choose another place to relax. Distance yourself from people who are negative and have destructive habits. Decide who you'll spend your free time with. There will be many times when you must endure negative people. Try not to spend time with them on purpose.

If you have dear friends you enjoy, but they are traveling a different road than you, limit your exposure. When you are with your negative friends, do not play into the drama of their lives. Empower them to enjoy your time together without entering a place of negativity or fear. Direct the conversation toward how they can change the situation by not giving power to it. Make it known through subtle actions that you will not tolerate the negativity and tragedy of their lives while you are with them. Listen to them as friends, give comfort and guidance, but set your barriers as to how far you will let them take you into the dissonance of their existence. Sometimes these friends will be healthier when they are with you, knowing that you do not want to live their dramas with them anymore. From others, you will have to detach completely to save your own sanity. You cannot attain peace if you always exist in the dramas of others.

Cleaning up your life is an important process if you wish to connect with bliss. Simplifying your schedule will give you the time to take care of the necessary tasks in your life. You have to cut from your routine things that do not serve your best interest. Sometimes deleting positive things is best, at least for a short time. You must clean and organize your home and workspace, as well as limit your exposure to negative people with destructive tendencies. The path to a blissful existence is sometimes not an easy journey. Tough choices have to be made and action must be followed through with determination. They say the journey is the destination, so if we can be peaceful while on the road to peace, we surely can be powerful and blissful people.

Bliss Technician Process:
Clean out the closet

Choose a closet in your home that is not perfectly organized. Allow yourself several hours to complete this task (this will save you a lot of time in the future). Take everything out of the closet, making piles of things that you could categorize together. For example, all of the shoes go together in one pile, all of the sports equipment in another, all of the jackets in another.

Except for seasonal things, if you haven't used something or worn it for a year, give it to charity. If you have two of something, you should give one away.

Before you put these items back in the closet, you may need to find shelves, cubbies, or even milk crates to help keep like items together. My closet has stacking shelves specifically made for shoes. I picked them up at a local department store, and they were inexpensive. Yard sales are always good for things like that as well.

"Calmness of mind is one of the
beautiful jewels of wisdom."

- James Allen

Chapter 7
Staying Calm

When we are in a state of calmness, our minds
are more prepared and open to connect with the bliss of
life. Stress and negative thinking shut down our senses,
disconnecting us from our inner peace. It's like shutting
all the windows and blinds in our homes on a beautiful
spring day. The sun may be shining, the flowers
blooming, birds are singing and a warm, fresh breeze is
blowing, but the stressful mind is blind to it all. Being
tense and agitated seems to disable our ability to see
positive outcomes and make intelligent choices.

When we are calm, we are able to make better
decisions. We are able to see situations clearer and
many possible positive outcomes become more evident.
In a state of calmness, we can quickly see through to the
end of a problem and take the most appropriate action.
When we live in a state of stress, we are unable to think
clearly or make educated decisions. We often make
mistakes that make matters worse. Why get stressed
when you have no control over others' actions and
external situations? It is much better to stay calm and
take appropriate actions for a more harmonious
outcome.

Staying calm when faced with adversity can be
learned and mastered, just as we have mastered
becoming stressed in tense situations. Being calm is just

a state of mind and emotion. You can direct how you act and how you are feeling. Martial artists are a great example of people who train themselves to be calm when faced with violence. Through actively thinking and training themselves, they strive to master the ability to be calm and react without fear or anger when attacked. The best martial artists stay so calm that they seem to avoid the very situations they are trained to combat. They exude calmness in everyday life and they often excel in difficult situations.

I was working as a professional ski patroller in the mid-nineties at Gunstock Ski Area in Gilford, New Hampshire. Often we would train to evacuate the chair lifts in case of a major breakdown. This is a tricky and dangerous procedure. We lower the people in the chairlifts to the ground with a specially made harness chair and ropes. Of course, sometimes we are in the chairlifts when they stop working, and we need to get down so we can help the other skiers to safety. In these cases we do what we call a "self-rappel" out of the lift.

I used to carry an emergency rappel rope, a sit-harness, a few carabiners and a figure eight in my backpack for such emergencies. If the lift stopped while I was on it, I would get my gear ready and rappel out of the chair. First, I would fasten my climbing harness snugly to my body. Then I would run my rappel rope slowly out of my pack until I had a few feet of slack touching the snow on the ground. The other end of the rope would go around the main support pole of the chair and then be lowered to the ground also. Once both ends were touching the ground, I would try to make them even. I would want to make sure each end was touching the ground with some slack. If one end were to accidentally slip through the rappelling gear, I would fall.

We do not tie the rope to the chair, so that we are able to pull it down after we are on the ground. If a rope is tied to the chair and the lift starts to move, it could cause a big problem. The rope could get caught up and derail the main cable, causing severe injury to the riders and massive damage to the lift. Looping the rappel rope over the center pole and not tying it off can be hazardous to the person rappelling. If the rope slips, or you do not run both ends through your figure eight, you will fall right to the ground.

A figure eight is exactly that—a smooth tube of aluminum molded in a figure eight. Climbers use figure eights to rappel by looping the rappel rope in and through it. The rope would go from a tie-down point (in this case, the main pole of the chairlift) through the figure eight and then to the ground. The friction of the rope passing through the figure eight and the weight of the person rappelling enables him or her to slowly control their decent to the ground. You have to make sure you loop the rope properly through the figure eight, or it will bind and you will be stuck hanging there.

My sit-harness was secure and the rope was properly hanging from the chair. I then fed the rope through my figure eight. This is awkward because you are sitting in a chairlift thirty or so feet above the ground with all your winter clothes on. When I thought I was ready to go, I raised the safety bar and scooted my way to the edge of the seat. I looked down at my co-workers and got the thumbs up; I smiled and popped out of the chair.

I instantly stopped about four feet below the chair. I had fed the rope through the figure eight backwards and was now stuck. My friends were in shock and bewilderment. Getting me back into the chair was not going to be easy, and it would be very time consuming. After I mentally yelled at myself for making such a foolish mistake, I knew I had to take action. The action I was thinking about was, well, insane. I closed my eyes and took a few deep breaths, and thought of my years of martial arts training. The mental conditioning to deal with stress and pain would surely come in handy at this moment. I knew my mind was calm and strong; the question was whether my body was able to physically pull it off. I hoped that my years of conditioning in the SEAL units would pay off.

I reached up with my left hand and firmly grabbed the bottom of the chairlift. I took a few more deep breaths and adjusted my grip until it felt right. With all the strength I could muster, I pulled myself up a few inches with my left arm, and with my right, I disconnected the rope and figure eight from my sit-harness. I heard someone yell, "What the hell are you doing? Are you insane?" Followed by a friend saying, "Shut up and let him concentrate. He can do it." I quickly put the figure eight in my mouth, as my left arm trembled under the pressure of holding me suspended under the chair. For a second, I though I was going to fall. I continued to control my breathing and intensely concentrate on the task at hand. With the figure eight clenched between my teeth, I swiftly re-looped the rope through it the correct way and reattached it to my harness. My left arm was throbbing in pain as I finally let go and safely rappelled to the ground.

The first thing I heard when I was down was my friend Joe yelling from another chair, "Man, that was sick!" Everyone gathered around to say they were worried I would fall, but I looked so calm and as if everything was going very well. My boss said I made an impossible task look easy—but not to ever do it again. I agreed.

When I was making the decision about what to do, I was not sure I would be able to hold on. As soon as I unhooked myself from the rope, I thought I had made a huge mistake. It was too late to think at that point. I had to stay calm not only for my sake, but for my friends and co-workers also.

I have found when you are centered and calm, you seem to project that onto others and the situation around you. Remember, stress is only a state of mind, and a situation is only temporary. You can look at a situation and see it in many ways. Everyone will react and interpret circumstances differently. Also, most people will look around to see how others are reacting and then follow. If you stay calm and centered, people around you will take your lead. Through your example, you can create a blissful capsule for everyone around you to take haven in.

I started my practice of being deliberately calm while driving my car. The roads and freeways of the world are a magnificent training ground for actively staying centered and calm. Sometimes it seems that people go out of their way to annoy and frustrate you while driving. It's as if getting behind the wheel of an automobile implies permission to be unsafe, aggressive, in a hurry and downright rude. Road rage has become a very serious problem in the U.S. We can use this problem on the highways for personal training and practice.

I have adopted a calm, forgiving and passive way of driving; I give way to all the scurrying people. I routinely wave someone past, let nudging cars in front of me and sometimes pull over to allow a tailgater to go ahead. I do this all with a smile, while I concentrate on how beautiful the day is. I give no energy to the aggressors of the road. I concentrate on my safe driving and my connection to the peaceful world I live in. It may seem funny, but even though I drive a rather large truck, I am passive while traveling. Ironically, I seem to always get to where I'm going at the same time as or just seconds behind the unruly speeder. The only noticeable difference is that I am calm and happy when I arrive, contrary to the frustrated state of the other driver.

It is so gratifying and peaceful to keep ourselves from falling prey to others' aggression and anger. Again, lead and teach by example. I know I do not want to teach my son that violence begets violence, but I do want him to know that there is strength and honor in choosing to be passive and non-confrontational. Is it not the stronger, wiser person who can smile, forgive and walk away? I always remember the teaching of the Buddha when faced with aggressive people.

It is told that the Buddha sat perched in lotus posture meditating under a tree when a disciple came to him. The follower was upset and disgruntled at the Master. He rudely yelled and voiced his opinions aggressively. After a few moments of yelling and receiving no response from the sage, the student asked, "What is the matter? Can't you hear me?"

The Buddha calmly looked into the eyes of his aggressor and said, "If I do not accept your gift of anger, does it not still make it your own?" The Buddha silently went back to meditation, and the boy humbly apologized and went away.

This lesson is powerful and can be life changing. If someone is angry, it does not mean you have to be angry too. By not allowing someone's aggression to affect you in a negative way, you instantly disarm the situation and assume the power position. This is what the Bible means regarding the meek inheriting the earth. A peaceful, calm person has much more inner power and strength than someone of anger and aggression. There is no greater example in history than that of Jesus. Jesus was the most powerful and influential person to ever walk the face of this planet. Jesus stayed calm and peaceful when faced with hostility and aggression, and it is said he never raised his voice or hand in anger.

You have the same choice that Jesus and the Buddha had when dealing with hostile people and situations. Stay calm and peaceful when faced with anger and aggression. Choose only to accept the gifts of love, harmony and forgiveness, and refuse offerings of hostility, anger and fear. When you are faced with adversity, choose a positive response. Breathe deeply and relax your body and your mind. Bring thoughts of joy and ecstasy into your mind and send love and forgiveness to everyone evolved. If you practice this whenever possible, living in the flow of bliss will be as normal and natural as breathing.

Bliss Technician Process:

Learning to concentrate on your breathing helps you to learn calmness and focus in many situations. First, sit comfortably and relax every muscle in your body. Start from the top of your head. Relax your eyebrows, eyes, and jaw, even your tongue. Relax the front of your neck, your shoulders, all the way to your toes. Now, only think of your breathing. Each time you inhale—completely fill your lungs. With each exhale—completely empty your lungs. Most of us fill our lungs only partially with each breath throughout the day. This is due to stress. This exercise will help you to train yourself to notice when you are doing this, and to be able to change it.

Also the lack of oxygen in the body from bad breathing habits can cause physiological stress on the body as well as contribute to mental stress. Proper breathing will ensure adequate oxygen levels in the body and brain.

"Don't compromise yourself. You are all you've got."

- Janis Joplin

Chapter 8
Be Yourself

You are incredibly powerful when you choose to be yourself and let your uniqueness show. Within each of us is a powerful and creative individual, with much to offer the world. We are all different. We all have different ideas and concepts of the universe and the world around us. That is part of the beauty of the self—its separateness and differences from others. Just imagine how the world would be if everyone were the same—dressed the same, thinking the same, liking the same things, having the same desires and goals. What a boring world we would live in!

Diversity is a wonderful spice of life and we should celebrate it. We should welcome the differences between us as wonderful miracles to be embraced and learned from. There is an amazing potential for all of us and it comes from our own personal ideas and ways of doing things. No two people are the same. Not even twins act and think alike. Outside, they may be identical, but within are two distinct individuals.

Most of us know that we are different and we want to express our uniqueness. Sometimes we feel others may look down upon us, so we repress our beautiful selves under layers of programmed responses and veils of indifference. This hiding of our natural empowering spirits diminishes us to a place of insecurity and doubt about our abilities and ourselves. This, of course, disconnects us from the bliss of life. The more we try to squelch our inner child from playing, the more depressed and repressed we become. It is so important to be yourself and understand the brilliance that is innate in all of us. Our creative and unique souls long to be set free and show us a blissful life that is truly ours to wander and explore.

So many times we get caught up in routines of social conditioning. We adopt the scripts of family, teachers, co-workers and friends. They too, long to let their true colors be seen. It is also true that misery loves company. It is a sad thing we do to each other when we attempt to manipulate and control others to be as repressed and insecure as we are.

As much as we are different, we all have this in common: at times, we just want to play. We want to explore and know the depths of wisdom and creation within and around us, but we feel trapped and worried about what others may think or say. We have conditioned ourselves that we should be constantly working, whether it's at a job or at home. Play is healthy. It's the reason elementary schools have recess—kids are more productive after a "play break." So take a recess! You can live that way or you can choose to live in your truth and let your amazing, distinctive self out of its shell and play.

Don't you find it odd that there is such a fine line between what we as a society, consider weird versus eccentric? Mostly, I find the difference is only whether one is famous or has lots of money. Think of it. Some very strange person who is very rich is said to be "eccentric," but if you were to act or dress in a similar fashion, people would call you "weird."

I often think of the differences in local musicians and popular rock stars. Just look at how the established rock star dresses and acts. We are all accustomed to their strangeness and odd ways of doing things. Just think of characters like Ozzy Osborne, Steven Tyler,

Madonna or Marilyn Manson. If they were to walk down our main street, people would think of them as eccentric. If you were to dress or act the same way, your friends would have you making an appointment with the local therapist! Why is that? It seems to me that the ones who follow their inner desires and let their unique souls shine somehow have a bigger impact in the world.

You should never be afraid to be yourself. If you are called odd or strange, consider it a huge compliment and know you're on the right track. True boredom is to follow the norm. Those who let their inner creative child live are always filled with wonder and enchantment and are truly connected with the bliss of life. They welcome "down time," for it is a time to think and create. Every one of us has a creative pulse. It is an important part of living a blissful life to let that child out. Explore what you have to offer yourself and the world. What is your creative inclination?

There are so many ways to let your uniqueness shine. You do not have to play an instrument or write a book. You can simply bake a cake, plant a garden or write a business plan. Think of a better way to make your office run more efficiently or redecorate your living room. There are many outlets for creativity. Find yours and let you individuality shine.

Being creative is more than just being an artist. You do not have to be an artist to be creative. My friend Scott is one of the most creative people I know, but he can't draw, paint, sing, write or play any instrument. He is amazing because of the ideas he has. His thoughts are utterly out of this world and he freely expresses himself through his creativity every day. Whether it's building a closet, repairing a boat, roofing a home or pulling a snowmobile out of a frozen lake, his ideas are always remarkable. Employees and customers sometimes do not understand what he is going to do, but the finished result is always miraculous.

"Be true to yourself and speak your mind. For the ones who matter the most will always accept you for who you truly are and the opinion of the others don't really matter at all"

Creativity means really being innovative and always trying new ways of doing things. Accepted, old ways have a long lineage of stability and the new ways are often criticized for the sake of not knowing what the outcome will be. Innovators are always thought of as odd and strange until they produce something amazing. Do you know the stories of Howard Hughes? Amelia Earhart? Bill Gates? The Wright Brothers? Christopher Columbus? Everyone thought these people were crazy and strange—until they succeeded. Then they were geniuses. I wonder why you have to get rich and famous with your creative, innovative endeavors for others to respect you. Is it because you have made money or is it because people are envious of the fact you followed you heart and dreams and, through your individual, creative side, made it good? I tend to believe the latter.

You don't have to invent time travel or win a Pulitzer Prize just be a creative pioneer in everyday life. Do not be afraid of looking foolish; consider it a compliment. Praise yourself for having the courage to try something new and let yourself be creative. Relish the joy of knowing you have made the choice to be yourself and let your imaginative child live through you. Welcome mockery and know that those people are only envious. Invite others to share in your innovative ventures and ideas and help allow the repressed souls around you to be set free. Set the example and it will be followed. Allow yourself to live in creative bliss, being a pioneer and an innovator of life.

Bliss Technician Process:

In your journal, write a proposal to a family member, a friend, or a co-worker about how to productively change a situation you are not happy with. In your proposal, state how everyone will benefit and be happier with the new way rather than with the old.

Write your proposal from a place of love and gratitude, sharing your inner feelings and thoughts. Be as specific as possible, as not to leave any room for speculation as to your motive. The goal of your proposal should be for the greater good of all, and not self serving.

Be able to back up your proposal with action, but do not expect or condemn others if they cannot see the glory of what you wish to accomplish. Know that you are a better person for even suggesting a better way to live.

"It isn't the experience of today that drives men mad.
It is the remorse for something that happened yesterday,
and the dread of what tomorrow may bring."

- Robert Jones Burdette

Chapter 9
Live in the Moment

There are many aspects of living a blissful life; however, being centered and living in the moment is surly one of the most powerful and life changing lessons to master. Can you imagine trying to walk three undisciplined dogs at the some time? What a task this would be, with all three animals pulling and prancing their own way. With one dog pulling you back, another thrusting forward, and one just sitting still, it would be nearly impossible to make any progress at all. Our thoughts can be as unruly and undisciplined as a pack of dogs, pulling and prancing their own way. Our focus seems to be moving in different directions. If we are focused on the past, letting what has transpired in our lives define who we are, or if our thoughts are held on what may or may not happen someday, we can never be centered in the moment and connect with the bliss of life. Too many people spend their lives paralyzed by the past or in fear of the future, or sometimes both. We have to learn that this moment is the time to live, and what is over or does not yet exist is nothing to be afraid of.

So many people dwell on past events or worry excessively about the future. There is no peace or harmony in living this way. You can paralyze yourself with the fears associated with the circumstances of past and future. Now, I know that the past may have been painful, but it is over—gone. The past is just a reflection of our minds, like an old movie we watched long ago. And like that old movie, it is just a memory, not a reality—unless you make it so by keeping it alive. You are not your memories; you are who you choose to be at this moment.

Your thoughts shape your reality. What you think and what you focus your thoughts on determines how you view and judge your life. If you are always thinking of the pain of the past or the fears of the future, you will forever be spiritually paralyzed. If the way you look at your life is painful, negative and fear-filled, then you will have a painful, negative and fear-filled life. It is a simple universal law: what you think about creates your current reality.

If you want to live a more productive, magnificent and blissful life, change the way you think to match what you desire. Think of things in a different light. Find the positive and optimistic outcomes for all situations—past, future and present. Change your thoughts to ones of empowerment and blissfulness. Eradicate your mind of negative and pessimistic thoughts. Empty the cup of your mind and fill it with joyous, peaceful and loving thoughts. In the absence of light, there is darkness, so fill your mind with light and cast the darkness of your life away.

This simple process of changing your thinking to create a better life may seem crazy, foolish or difficult to you. You may even think the idea is too simplistic to make a difference. It is powerful and will work if you optimistically commit to the process. Let me give you an example of how changing my thoughts about my past freed me from destructive patterns and led to a more fulfilling relationship with my father.

Throughout my life I had always lived in the shadow of my father's stern hand, striving to live up to his standards and gain his approval. As a child, nothing I ever did seemed good enough for him. So I tried harder and strived to be more perfect in his eyes. With every step I took, I was ridiculed, put down and led to believe nothing I did was ever good enough.

I kept trying to attain perfection so that I would be noticed and accepted by my father. This behavioral pattern continued into adulthood, shaping my decisions and my life. I was always angry with my situation in life and my relationship with my father was very poor.

As time went by, I pondered my childhood and realized the incredible lessons I had learned from my dad. I came to see him as someone who tried to make me the best at everything I did only because he wanted the best for me. He taught me not to be satisfied with average, but to shoot for the stars and be the best I could be always. As I looked back on those powerful lessons, I came to know I would not have been able to do all the wonderful things in my life if those lessons had not been learned.

I was then grateful to my father for being himself and doing all that he knew to make me one who always strives to be the best, and to never settle for less than I want. Realizing the truth of my childhood released the angers and frustrations of current life and moved my relations with my father to a higher, positive level.

Living in the past can be paralyzing, but with practice and actively directing our thoughts, we can be free of those pesky chains that hold us back from connecting with the bliss of life.

Why fear what is yet to happen? We do not know what will transpire. If we had a daily guidebook of everything coming our way, would we really be better off? What would be the fun in living if there were no mystery, no adventure? There's profound wisdom in knowing that *right now* is the only time you have. At this moment, you are alive. At this moment, you have the ability to choose your every action and reaction. At this moment, you are in control of your existence. We should experience all of this moment and savor its very existence. This is blissful living.

So many people live in the fear of what may happen to them. They create all sorts of hypothetical situations and let those illusions control their decisions and their lives. The thing is, whether something bad or good will come to fruition someday is no reason to not be happy and blissful today. No matter what will happen, why not just be relaxed and harmonious now? And better yet, why not just choose to be in a state of bliss, regardless of your surrounding situation, good or bad?

You can "what if" yourself into a stressful, unhealthy mind-frame, where you fear to try anything new or move forward with your life. You have to know that your future is an empty slate, waiting for you to live in the story. By connecting with the bliss of life, knowing that peace and harmony are only a thought away and a choice you make, you can face the uncertainty of the future with open arms.

The future is unwritten, unknown, so all the drama surrounding what will happen in your life is useless, because you have no idea what will transpire. You do know, however, that life is uncertain, and in that uncertainty is the adventure worth living. Embrace the knowledge that nothing is known, and that you have total control of your reaction and responses to every situation in your life.

Change your thoughts from ones of thinking "something may happen" to realizing you do not know what will happen. There is a certain peace and strength in this knowledge. Blissfulness comes from not knowing what will happen but knowing you are okay right now. With every passing moment, you are okay.

When I closed my business, I lost my source of income. I did not know what would happen. I did not know if I would ever actually publish a book and be a speaker. I did not even know what I wanted to write about. I just closed my business and moved forward into the unknown. I eradicated all negative, hypothetical thoughts and kept my blissful center— knowing I was fine that day, even if I did not know what would happen tomorrow. I concentrated on my task and I wrote every day. Mostly I just wrote my thoughts on paper, until one day I realized I was living in a state of bliss.

I realized the power and essence of being blissful for the day and not worrying about the unknown future. Hence, this book and the associated workshops were born. Through my blissful mindset— knowing I am okay right now—I was able to take the action steps daily towards changing my career and my life.

Accept the essence of this moment as the only time you have. Breathe it in with the knowledge that everything is okay right now, at this very moment. As you exhale, release the fears and false stories of the future and connect with the bliss of knowing nothing is really known.

What is in the past does not exist and can no longer hurt you. Similarly, what lies in the future does not exist either, so it too cannot do you any harm. The only time you should look at is right now. Are you okay right now? Then what's the problem?

Bliss Technician Process:
Giving thanks

Look around and notice all the blessings in your life. In your journal, make a list of everything good in your life right now. Some things can be as simple as the fact that you have a hummingbird to watch outside, or that your African Violet has finally decided to blossom! List everything you have to be thankful for, especially the good people in your life.

No matter what your situation is, be thankful for what you have and not what is lacking. The fact that you wake every morning and have the capacity to choose how to live each day is a blessing enough!

"Be happy in the moment - that's enough.
Each moment is all we need - not more."

- Mother Teresa

Chapter 10
Life is Perfect Right Now

The grass is not always greener on the other side of the fence. It is only a perception in the fields of your mind as to what is green or brown. Until you can actually walk in the shoes of your neighbor, you will never know if he truly is happy or better off than you are. In most cases, I have found they are peering over the fence, looking at your "great life" as something they aspire to attain.

You really don't know what you have until it is gone. In the absence of what was, you find a certain appreciation for your life and, sometimes, a longing to have parts of it back. It is very important to take an inventory of everything in your life and to see that, even if you do not have much, you are blessed with many wonderful things. Blissful people are thankful for the things they have, and do not regret or pine over what they do not.

Jack had a good life. He ran a popular convenience store in his hometown. He made good money and had the freedom to come and go as he pleased. When he started getting frustrated with his business life, he looked to others' lives as a source of aspiration. He became more frustrated and disgruntled as he looked at every get-rich-quick scheme he could waste his money on. He started to hate working for himself and he lost the sense of freedom his business had formerly given him.

Finally, the universe answered his requests. Another company took control of his store and forced him out. Faced with the reality that he would soon be without his business, he tried to fight for it back. His efforts only brought more frustration, stress and a quickly dwindling bank account. For a long time he sat on the couch, unemployed, depressed and longing for the freedom and status he once had had. His finances toppled and his family life and home was also in jeopardy. He realized how good he had actually had it, but it was gone.

If you are always focused on what you do not have—on what you lack in life—then the universal law of attraction will bring you *more* of that emptiness. When you think of all you do not possess, you will subconsciously put yourself in situations that will produce more of what you do not have.

Jack, the storeowner, only concentrated on what he did not have and the universe responded promptly. Sometimes, it is not until we can embrace the beauty in our current lives—no matter what our situations may be—that we can move on to a higher level of being. By continually focusing on all the negative aspects in our lives, we subconsciously keep ourselves in that dissonant place. We may actually become comfortable living in that place, partaking of the materialistic pleasures, which momentarily make us feel better. We make living in negativity a bad habit, continually brought on by our thought processes.

Like any bad habit, negative thinking can be broken. You first have to identify the negative mind-set that is holding you back. You must realize you chose to live disconnected from the flowing bliss of life and you can make a decision to plug into it at any time. At this moment, you can choose to connect with the natural bliss of life. It's your choice. How do you want to live?

After a painful time, Jack finally did a thorough inventory of his life. With help and support from close friends and family, he made a list of what he was actually good at and what made him happy. He realized he did love working for himself and he had a talent for building and remodeling homes. Jack made a choice to get off the couch and save his life and his marriage. He realized how good he had it and began to recognize all the wonderful people in his life who were loving and supportive, especially his wife. He recaptured his essence and went into business as a carpenter. His love for his new business and his innate talents as a builder soon gave him a great and fast-spreading reputation. Within a few short years, he had substantially grown his company and is now one of his hometown's premier homebuilders.

Jack realized all the wonderful things he was capable of and how lucky he was to have such a supportive, loving wife. When he finally broke the chains of the past, moved through the fears of the future and lived in the moment, taking control of the only time he had, Jack transformed his life beyond his expectations.

When you realize "the now" is where we all live—not in the past or future—you can connect with the bliss of life and become calmer and more peaceful. When you find the courage and power to direct your life toward you dreams and desires every moment of every day, your life becomes an amazing, blissful adventure.

Bliss Technician Process:

Constant learning is an important ingredient for living a blissful life. This may take time and some planning. In your journal, make a list of things you'd like to learn over the next year. The list should include classes or lessons you'd like to take, such as pottery, self defense, kayaking, skiing, photography or hang-gliding as well as things you could teach yourself, such as gardening, nutrition, a musical instrument, painting or weaving. Be very specific. Investigate the cost of learning each thing (how much does a pottery class at your local potter's cost?) How long will it take? What else will you need? (You might need books or supplies). After each item, write these things down. Then write when you'll do it. How will you make it fit into your schedule? How will you pay for it? Remember not to overload your schedule. If you can only take one class this year, that's fine. By constantly learning, you'll be growing not only mentally, but spiritually as well.

Books are a great way to learn. Sometime in the next week, go to a bookstore or library and look for a book on a subject that interests you. Read this book, and when you are done, go find another one. One should always have a book in progress.

"Optimism is the faith that leads to achievement.
Nothing can be done without hope or confidence."

- Helen Keller

Chapter 11
Watch your thoughts

Our thoughts have a powerful impact on how we view the world and the circumstances we find ourselves in. We have the power within us to create our situations and bring into our lives what we truly desire. Through positive thinking and intention, we can deliberately sway our actions and views of peace, love and harmony. We give energy to whatever we think about. The process within our minds—the inner story that constantly runs in the background of our thoughts—has a dramatic effect on the outcome of our lives.

Our thoughts are like powerful magnets, pulling toward us what we concentrate on. The more we hold a thought in our minds, the more powerful is the magnetic pull that will draw that situation into our lives.

Whatever we constantly think of—whether it is negative and destructive or empowering and uplifting—we will bring into our lives the very situation we concentrate on. There is a powerful universal force that flows through all of us. This force has many names, depending on your beliefs and religion. Whatever you call it—God, Brahma, Buddha, the universe, or source—it is one of giving, abundance and constant supply. The only catch is, this ever-giving source gives to us anything and everything we hold our thoughts on—whether it is positive or negative.

Have you ever sat back and wondered why some people seem to be lucky all the time and some are always getting the short end of the stick? Look at the type of thought and talk that these different people have. You will find the one with the happy, positive outlook is the one with good luck, and the one who is focused on the negative all the time inevitability seems to have bad luck. Luck, whether good or bad, has nothing to do with it. It is the concentration of thoughts, good or bad, which dictate the circumstances in our lives.

The universal energy within you does not understand the difference between lack and negativity and abundance and harmony, it only knows to give us what we ask for. We ask all the time—by what we think and concentrate on. If we always concentrate and talk about the negative aspects and loss in our lives, the universe will then send us more negativity and loss. Even if we hold thoughts of not having these insufficiencies in our lives, source will only hear the "insufficiencies" in our inner dialogue. It is impossible to connect with the bliss of life if we continually hold negative and pessimistic thoughts in our minds.

My friend, James, is a good example of someone who is always focused on the negative when it comes to women. Every time we talk about meeting women, his story line is disheartening and pessimistic. As we talk, he says things like, "I would like to meet a nice girl, but I only meet unattractive ones who I have nothing in common with" or "I would like to ask this girl I met last week out, but she won't like me because I'm too old for her and I'm overweight." Lately, he has been projecting his negativity outward and blaming women for his shortcomings. He told me the other day he is getting very good at lying. He believes he should tell women what they want to hear in order to get what he wants.

James thinks women are liars and are only after one thing: money. He mentally sets himself up for failure before be even gets going. He has such a negative vibe about him when it comes to women that they really do not find him attractive or interesting at all. In fact, he is very smart, intelligent and interesting. He is a great guy who is financially secure and he is good-looking. His self-sabotaging, negative outlook destines him to being alone. When he does finally meet up with someone, she tends to have ulterior motives and be after his money. Of course—this is what he asks for by constantly thinking about it!

Think of universal source as a powerful metal detector. It will find scrap or gold, but you have to set the meter. This is where it gets tricky. If the switch on the meter is in the "FIND SCRAP" position or set for "NO SCRAP," the focus is still on SCRAP—so you will always find scrap. By holding the intention and thought in your mind of NOT finding scrap, you send out scrap vibrations. You are thinking of scrap, not gold. Remember, the universe does not know about "not" and "don't," it only knows what we are asking for. The universal ear does not hear the NOT in your request, it only hears what you asked for, which is scrap. You would have a better chance of striking it rich if you set you selector switch to "I never find GOLD." This way, the universe hears "Gold" and will give it to you.

This may be a hard concept to understand at first. With practice and patience, you will learn to understand how your thoughts create realities and, ultimately, how to control what comes into your life by focusing your thoughts. If you want to live a more fulfilling, peaceful life, you have to think of being fulfilled and peaceful. If you want to connect with the bliss of life, you first have to think you are already in the flow.

The trick in dealing with thought and universal energy is to always think of what you want in a positive way. To really bring abundance, joy and harmony into your life and live completely in bliss, you must think about it optimistically. You must set your selector switch to what you want. Do not focus on loss and disharmony. When you focus on what you do not want, you continue to create the same situation in your life. Focus on what you do want, and you will see a change.

For me one of the best lessons of the power of thought and self-fulfilling prophecy was when I was just about to start Navy SEAL training. I was in a group of about 130 men who were going to start the most grueling military training in the world. Statistics said less than 25% of us would make it beyond "Hell Week," a phase of training where we would not sleep for six days and would be constantly on-the-go physically. I remember predicting who would make it and who would quit, just by listening to the way they talked with each other.

Whether they were confident and strong or not, I believed their thoughts would ultimately dictate whether they would make it. If I heard someone talking about "not being a quitter," or saying "I'm not going back to the fleet Navy again," or "I won't fail," and "I won't get hurt," they were soon gone. They were holding the intention of what they wanted and source heard the thoughts of "quitter," "fleet," "fail" and "hurt," because that was, ultimately, what they were concentrating on.

My group of friends made it, not because we were stronger or better in any way than those who dropped out or failed. Only our mind-sets differed. I concentrated on being a SEAL and finishing training. I thought of my success and focused on culminating the training strong and healthy. When things got tough, I would think of making it through each training evolution. I concentrated on the fact that I volunteered for this training, and no matter how hard it got, it was much better than pumping gas or washing dishes back in my hometown. Truthfully, I did not know if I would be able to finish the training, I only hoped I would. My thoughts were always focused on a positive outcome in a positive way. This was true for all my friends who graduated training and went on to be SEALs. The universe answered our intentions of "completion," "graduation" "healthy" and "being a SEAL"—just as we thought!

It is important to evaluate your thought processes to see if your mind-set is predisposed to being negative or positive. Again, you bring into your life what you hold in your thoughts, so negative thinking brings more negative circumstances into your life.

It is not an easy task, but a very worthy one, to re-train your mind to deliberately think positively and hold thoughts of what you want and desire. It is even more powerful to think as if these good things have already happened or are happening in your life. I do not mean to delve into a delusionary state of existence, letting fantasy reign. However, you can realistically think of what you want as coming to you and manifesting in your life at this moment. You may not have it, but you KNOW it is going to happen. Focus your thoughts to think of the things you would like in your life, as if they were happening and evolving in the moment. Remember that the bliss of life flows around and through you at all times. It is within your power whether to connect or disconnect from it.

There is a glint of realism in the phrase "fake it till you make it." If you act as if circumstances and situations in your life are as you want them to be, you will automatically focus your thoughts in a positive way. You will show the universe exactly what you want to bring into your life and, through positive and constructive thinking, you will magnetize what you want and draw it to you.

For years, I was running my business alone, working seven days and well over 75 hours a week. I complained that I could not find any good employees to help me out. I put ads in the local and regional papers. I tried head-hunters and internet job sites. I offered incentives and paid training, however, I could never find any qualified help.

I negatively focused on the fact I had no help for several years, and I was quickly burning out. As my busy season came upon me, I knew I could not work at that pace anymore and the thought of closing my shop entered my mind. I decided I would only work 40 hours a week and cut back my teaching schedule. This choice eased my mind and I started to think positively about the busy season. I began to think how nice it would be if I could find a qualified scuba instructor to work full-time. This would free up my nights and weekends and enable me to enjoy a bit of the summer time, which I had been missing for close to seven years.

I remember telling people I was going to find a full-time, qualified person to teach, and if not, I would only teach when I had the extra time. It was not stressful to me, since I had already made the decision to work less. Finding someone to teach would be a bonus.

With my new plan, I became excited about finding the right person to do the job. I found myself relishing the thought of sitting at home in my back yard relaxing while someone else was covering the store for me. These thoughts made me happy and more determined to find that special employee. I began to make plans for time off and trips to the ocean with friends. I thought of all the hikes and camping trips I could take. I planned to kayak a few mornings a week, and would start to ride my bike again. I still had ads in the papers and on the internet.

One day I got an email from a certified scuba instructor who lived in Vermont, only a few hours away. He wanted to work for me, and drove down to meet me. I hired him on the spot and he proved to be the answer to my prayers. I had an incredible summer, as he took up more than his share of the business responsibilities.

Faced with the same dilemma the next season, after my star employee moved to Florida, I started my positive thinking regime again. That year I manifested a highly motivated college girl who was a selling machine. With almost no training, she excelled at all aspects of running my business. I taught all the classes at night and on the weekends, and had all my weekdays free. She agreed to return the following year. I began to think how great it would be if I had an instructor along with her. I thought about what a beautiful summer I would have. I could take the entire season off and let them run my shop together.

A few weeks after I began my fantasy of not working for the first time in 10 years, I got a call from an instructor in England who wanted to come to New Hampshire and work for the summer. When I hired him, my dream of having a summer off was fulfilled. Jessica and Charlie were a great team—the best thing that ever happened to my business. I had a great summer. But, unfortunately, they both left at the end of the season. They were such a great team that they got engaged to each other and left for greener pastures!

To demonstrate how powerful thought can be— good or bad—let me tell you what happened the next year. After Jess and Charlie left, I was devastated. I could not handle my shop alone. They had enabled me to grow my business ten-fold in two years. I could not control it myself anymore. I was scared I would not find anyone to work the next season. I started to think how terrible it was going to be with no trained sales people or instructors. Spring came and I was employee-less! I could not focus positively on a good outcome for the season, and it went very poorly for me. My sales in the shop were more than 30% down and I could not keep a handle on the classes. I taught half of the former year's certifications for diving! I had slipped into negative thinking habits regarding finding employees—and none came!

It is so important to be optimistic and think positively. If you do, amazing things will happen to you—sometimes things you do not even think of happening, but when you expect good things to happen all the time, they will.

Again, do not delve into a delusion and just sit on the couch thinking things will be more blissful. You have to take action and be realistic as to what you desire. It is not magic, but intention and determination that will bring glorious things your way. I have found that when you train your thoughts to be empowering and positive and connect with the bliss of life, many doorways open for you. They might not be exactly what you want, but will be more than you need at the moment. When you stay positive and focused on peace and harmony, you will naturally be open to suggestions and the opportunity to enhance your life. You will find you notice synchronistic events and situations unfolding before you. When you choose to connect with the bliss of life and let your spirit lead you, people and things will appear in your path to enhance your circumstances. The following story illustrates exactly what I mean.

Janis found herself alone with her nine-month-old baby boy. She was in a new, unfamiliar town in Texas, and her husband had been deployed to Iraq. Although her husband's paycheck supported the bare necessities, she needed to find a job.

Janis is a very active person and staying at home every day, without any extra money to enjoy her life was making her depressed and discouraged. College-educated with a Nursing Degree, she was certain she could find a job on the army base, which would be close to home and her son's daycare. She had been told that securing a job on the base was nearly impossible. For months, she incessantly tried to get a nursing position on or near the base, but she always ended up at a locked door. She was very frustrated and stressed. She thought of leaving Texas to move back to Colorado where she could find suitable work and had many friends.

Overwhelmed, Janis called me for advice. We talked about her baby and how much she loved being a mom. Reminiscing about our high school days and old friends lightened her mood a bit. As we talked she began to realize she was okay at the moment. She had begun to harbor negative thoughts. She had disconnected herself from her natural blissful state and became pessimistic. She kept saying she'd never get a job on the army base. I suggested she change her focus from finding a nursing job to finding any job. She just needed a part-time job to redirect her energy and get her out of the house a few days a week. We talked about finding a stress-free, fun job where she could make new friends and a few extra bucks. Centered and with renewed confidence, Janis agreed this was a good idea and she set out to find a suitable, fun job.

A few weeks later, Janis called me, very excited. She had gone out and interviewed with several businesses she thought would be fun places to work and an amazing thing had happened. During an interview, she told a woman about her desire to work on the base as a nurse. She explained she had been unable to find the right person to interview with, so she had decided to find a fun job instead. She knew that eventually she would run into the right person, but for now she needed a job for her sanity. Although the woman wanted to hire her, she said she knew someone who knew the hiring director of the base hospital. Janis was ecstatic when her new friend was able to get her the number. The following week, she interviewed and was hired to work as a nurse at the base hospital!

When Janis replaced her frustration and stress with hope and excitement, the world unfolded in front of her. She knew she would eventually work at the hospital, and she kept those thoughts in the forefront of her mind. She became peaceful and centered with that knowledge, and she was happy to work somewhere else until that day came.

Thought plays such an important role in how we see and live our lives. The power of thought as a means to change your life is vastly underrated. You can direct and create your life according to your mind-set and thought patterns. If you can change the way you think of the world, the world around you will surely change as well. Choose your thoughts wisely. Stay positive and focus on what you truly desire in your life. Connect with the bliss of life by holding thoughts of peace and joy in your mind. Your life can be amazing, so make it happen.

Bliss Technician Process:

Think of your life as if you were completely connected with bliss. Visualize how your life would be if you were in peace and harmony all the time, without stress or worry. In your journal, write about how beautiful and gratifying life would be. Write about how you would react to negative situations in your life.

How would your connection to bliss affect and help the people and loved ones around you? How would you feel? What would your life be like? Write it all down. Capture the perfection of your life as it is when completely connected with the bliss of life. After you have finished, take a moment to read what you have written. As you meditate for a few moments on this foreseeable you, create a Bliss Box to capture the essence and moment of what you aspire to. Place this Bliss Box on a shelf in your mind, and routinely open it throughout your day. The more you connect with the positive essence of what you want, the closer it comes to being there in reality.

"Perceive and rejoice that life is abundant;
that beauty and goodness are amply available;
that your happiness is in your hands."

- Paul Hodges

Chapter 12
Seek to See the Best

My life is far from sensational or glamorous, as I write this book. I am living in a middle-class neighborhood with a modest income. I am a single parent of a three-and-a-half year old son. I run a scuba diving shop and a barge service company. I am not monetarily wealthy. In fact, I have no savings or retirement at all. I live from month-to-month, never knowing how much business I will do. But there is one thing that separates me from others in similar situations: my mind-set.

Some see my life as chaotic, but I have a different view altogether. Although my schedule is frenzied at times, I am in a calm, harmonious state—most of the time anyway—and I give thanks for all that I have. Some say I am just lucky, but I know luck has nothing to do with it. I have worked very hard for everything in my life. I have transcended thoughts of luck, knowing I am blessed by the heavens and my success is brought on by my actions and not by accident. I look at my life as divine and exactly what I need at any moment in time. I stay centered in thoughts of how great my life is and that I have everything I need and lack nothing. I do know I have a mission in this life and I know I will soon be in a different place, so I savor the moment and try to learn the lessons I need to evolve spiritually, emotionally and physically. If I had been in any other situation, I would not have had the time or resources to write this book and change my life.

I choose empowering, uplifting thoughts over negative, destructive ones. Of course, it took me a long time to realize and clearly see the pessimistic, controlling and caustic lifestyle I was absorbed in. As I entered early adulthood, I developed a mind-set of negative reinforcement to keep myself going and on top of the game. Although it seemed to work on the outside and I did accomplish many things and visited lots of interesting places, I was always frustrated and unhappy with my place in life. I was anything but connected to the bliss of life, and I always saw the negative side to every situation.

I was deployed in Europe with SEAL Team Two in the late '80s. Many of my SEAL team-mates were having the time of their lives visiting all the Mediterranean ports. The food, the culture and the women were the talk of the breakfast table on most mornings. My friends saw the deployment as a chance to explore and have fun. I had a different view altogether. For most of the seven-month tour, I stayed on the ships or naval bases and trained. I saw the deployment as work, and since I was a Navy SEAL, my job was to be combat ready 100% of the time. While my friends were diving in the Red Sea, I stayed on the ship and cleaned my weapons. When many of my platoon members took a weekend to go to Rome and Florence, Italy, I stayed on the ship in Naples inspecting all the scuba gear. While at port in Spain, my friends would go out on the town, shopping, sightseeing and meeting European women, but I stayed back doing hundreds of pushups, sit-up and pull-ups. I would routinely leave the ship, but only to go for a run or a swim for training.

I knew our chances of going on a dangerous, real-life mission were very high since we had been put on stand-by many times. I began to think poorly of some of my fellow SEALs; I thought they were not truly ready for a challenging mission. I began to focus on all the holes in the plans and our platoon, and thought the only way I would make it out alive is if I were in extremely good physical condition. I had become a pessimist. I only saw the downside of every situation. I was always in a bad mood and upset with my friends for having so much fun. Really, the problem was not my friends having fun; they were all competent and highly trained SEALs. The problem was that I thought they should not be enjoying themselves—they should be training as hard as I was. I thought my life was a daunting chore, and theirs were not. I wasted seven months of my life staring at the steel deck of a ship, while I could have been exploring and enjoying what the coastal countries of the Mediterranean had to offer. I could not see the positive side to my circumstances, and I paid for it with my misery.

When my deployment was over, my time in the Navy was up and I was honorably discharged. My life as a SEAL was over, but the pessimism and negative mind-set stayed with me for years.

I continued to concentrate on the possible failures and the contingency plans to avoid such failings. This may not have been a bad business strategy and it got me through college on the dean's list, but the absorption of my thoughts of failure cultivated deep-seated fears of attempting success.

During my early thirties, I found myself a shell of a man, hiding in the obscurity and comfort of not trying so I wouldn't fail. This was, to me, implacable logic: If I do not attempt anything, how can I fail? I was miserable and bliss was only an illusion.

I sometimes wonder how I fell into that mind-set, after all the things I had done in my earlier years. But as people get older, the childish enthusiasm to attempt endeavors just for the sake of having the experience can transform into the fear of social rejection. Instead of thinking of the fun and adventure you may have, you worry about your social standing when you consider whether you will succeed or fail and what level of achievement you might attain. Basically, you are more concerned with what others will think of you for doing something and what will be said of you if you fail, than you are with creating a blissful, fulfilling life. Self-doubt and worry disconnects us from the flow of bliss, leading the way to frustration and misery.

I know this was true in my case. I harvested only the negative aspects of my life in my mind. I saw only the downside of my existence and the grass always looked greener on the other side of the fence. I was so preoccupied looking to others and elsewhere for acceptance and happiness that I could not see how beautiful and blessed my life really was. I finally realized I was the source of my well-being and happiness. I was connected to everything and everybody, and it was only my thoughts that dictated how I perceived the situations of my life. My destiny was in my control, and I had the choice of how to live my life. I came to that realization after watching a movie called *Excalibur*.

At that point, I was running my scuba diving store for about seven years and was very weary and frustrated with its performance. I was pessimistic and negative about almost everything. In my opinion, my business did not generate enough money and I was working well over 70 hours a week for little gratification. My friends and acquaintances seemed to be doing so much better than I was. Everyone around me appeared to be so happy and having so much fun, I wondered what my problem was. I would complain to friends, but they would only look at me funny and say they wished they had my life. I dismissed their responses as nonsense.

I set out to find out what I could do to make my life happier, less busy and more profitable. I fell prey to the many business schemes out to sell the ideal to weary souls. I wasted a lot of money and time on several of these dead-end endeavors.

I tried to market several multi-level marketing/pyramid business ideas. I bought into the idea I would get my friends into selling vitamins and skin care products and I would make a ton of money. Instead, I alienated my friends. I lost lots of time trying to cold-sell people. I lost a lot of money buying senseless products. As if that wasn't enough, I then bought into the 900-number business idea, foolishly dropping a large sum of cash to get the business started. I was told I would make thousands a week, but I only lost every dime I put into the idea. For years, I bought into every infomercial boasting instant millionaire status, only to lose money on each venture. As I concentrated my efforts on trying to get rich quick, my business went down the toilet, and I was still miserable and unfulfilled.

On that day, I sat on top of one of my favorite hiking hills, looking out over the beautiful Lake Winnipesaukee. I fell into a peaceful place for a moment. I wondered if things were not that bad for me after all. I did have my own business. Although it was small, it did provide for me. I had a new vehicle every three years. I lived alone, while many of my peers needed roommates. I had enough money to go out several nights a week, and I took at least three vacations a year. I began to see what my friends told me. My life was pretty good, and it was only me who saw it differently.

I began to think about why my business was not working as well as I wanted it to, and why it was so much work to keep it running. I lay back on a rock with the sun warmly shining upon my face and I fell asleep. I awoke with a thought lingering in my mind. I remembered a scene from the movie *Excalibur* where, after years of blight and famine in the land of King Author, Percival came with the elusive message of the Holy Grail.

As the land and King Arthur lay dying simultaneously, Percival's words rang clearly in the King's ear: "You and the land are one, Sire." When you are sick, the land falls ill, when you are well, the land thrives. So, as King Arthur rose above his doubts and fears and realized that he and the kingdom were one, he transformed the impoverished land into a thriving empire once again.

I realized that, in the same sense, I was my business. How I thought about it and the energy I put into it was reflective of how my business would be. I then realized how lucky I was to have created such a great job. Even though it was not my life's ultimate purpose, it served as a learning place and afforded me the time to grow and search for my identity.

With this knowledge came harmony and bliss in working my business. I had a new-found respect for my life and viewed it as productive and blessed, rather than enslaving and mundane. And as I focused my energies on running my business in a positive way, my work rewarded me with more income and more time off to enjoy life. I discovered the secret of my own Holy Grail.

This concept works the same for every situation, including your life. You are your life, and the way you think about it is how it will be. If you think your life is miserable, you will find misery everywhere you look. If you believe your life is blessed and encompassed by peacefulness and harmony, you will find yourself connecting with the bliss of life every day.

Seek to see the best in everyone and every situation. This is the only real control we have. Our outlook has such a powerful effect on how our lives play out. We disconnect ourselves from the bliss of life by focusing on the negative. When we are able to train our minds to see the true nature of ourselves, others and the world, we will see there is a positive side to every situation. Even the most trying and negative circumstances have an upside. Sometimes we cannot understand why there are so many cruel people and such harsh things happening in the world. We cannot control these people or things. We can only decide how to respond. We can be dragged down and assume a negative outlook, or we can seek bliss within ourselves. We can try to understand how and why the world operates, but we have to remember we did not create it: God did.

The true reason and nature for all that exists is beyond our comprehension. Since we are all created in the likeness of God, then there must be a reason for everything: good and bad. It is not our mission to judge what is happening, only to look upon others with compassion, forgiveness and love. Every situation we encounter is an opportunity to learn and grow. We transform when we are able to see the good in everyone and every situation without judgment. A Course in Miracles defines a miracle as a transformation from a thought system based on fear to one based on love.

If we are able to see the world through loving eyes and not fear-filled illusions, we will be able to see the best in everything. A homeless person begging on the street is a chance to show compassion, not to pass judgment. Even a murderer should be looked upon with mercy. While we should never forget the act, we can show forgiveness. This is an extreme example, but we are faced with these situations, and sometimes it is next to impossible to see the bright side. This is when we truly can transform to a higher lever of consciousness and live a more blissful life.

Bliss Technician Process:

Think of three people and three situations in your life that you think are negative or bad. In your journal, write five reasons why you think this. For each person, write ten positive things about them. It can be anything as long as it is optimistic and positive. Do the same for each negative situation. As you read over your journal and focus on the positive side of these people and situations, can you feel a shift in your opinion? Write about this shift, whether good or bad.

For example: Last year a drunk driver hit me head on. I was not hurt badly, but my truck was very damaged. I was without a vehicle for almost six weeks, and it cost several thousand dollars to fix it. When I finally got it back, it did not work right. It had many glitches that were not there before. Instead of focusing on the negative aspects of the situation, I started thinking maybe it was time for a new truck. A few months later, my truck broke down in the dead of winter, stranding my son and me out in the cold. Again, I focused on the positive and within two weeks I purchased a new truck. I did not really like my old truck, so the accident was a blessing. I was able to find the truck I wanted and felt good about it. My new truck is much better suited for family, personal and business use.

"The genius of communication is the ability to be totally honest and totally kind at the same time."

- James Powell

Chapter 13
The Importance of Communication

We cannot go through life alone. Those who try to stand alone fall fast. To face life unaccompanied is to delve deeply into fear and doubt. Isolation is known to make a person go insane. We were put on this earth together for a reason. We need each others' love and support as we face the trials and lessons of existence. No matter who you are or what your place in life, there is someone who has been or is there who understands you and can offer support and help. We are blessed with a world of people, who, in my experience, are always ready to lend an ear and helping hand if needed. Having a healthy network of helping companions brings joy and harmony to anyone's life.

You would not be reading this book if it wasn't for the support of a few great friends. As I set out to change my life and become a writer and speaker, I found myself alone. When I shared my intentions with my family and some close friends, I hoped for encouragement and understanding. Instead I got silence. Suddenly I felt so alone, and the book seemed overwhelming. For three months I struggled to get through the first three chapters. I thought maybe I was a fool to attempt such a project.

I heard of an empowerment course for aspiring spiritual writers, taught by Dr. Doreen Virtue and Dr.

Steven Farmer. I signed up and was on my way to Laguna Beach, California.

During the course I was glad to find so many others in the same position I was—aspiring writers with no direction or support. I learned a lot and developed close friendships with several people in the group. The weekly phone calls and email exchanges were the foundation I needed to keep my spirits high and to complete this book. Within two months of returning from Laguna Beach, I completed the manuscript.

Not only is facing life with the companionship of others necessary, it is fun and uplifting and you are able to produce and experience so much more. Sharing your failures and successes with others is gratifying and uplifting and it gives you the strength to continue exploring the endless adventures that life has to offer. With support and the bliss of knowing you are not alone, your potential is unlimited.

When I think of the potential that lies within strong relationships, the example of my experience with the Navy SEALs comes to mind.

In the special warfare community, we refer to ourselves as "the Teams." We refer to ourselves as Team Guys, not SEALs. We are taught that there is no "ME" or "I" in the word TEAM. Without each other, there is no possible way the mission could be accomplished at all. Everyone has a specialty; everyone is unique. We all have our fears and weaknesses. We operate as one unit of individuals. Together, we are unstoppable and what we can do as a unit is beyond belief.

Take any one SEAL out of the sanctuary of his platoon to perform tasks that would be seemingly easy within the cohesiveness of his unit and you will be amazed at the inadequacy of his abilities. Where did all this potential go? Nowhere, it is still there. He is still a SEAL, just not in his team. A lone Team Guy is just that, alone. The Hollywoodification of the "Rambo" type is misleading. It implies that one guy can do it alone. The actual Rambo movie was quite the opposite in message. He was alone, afraid, walking with fear and doubt. Without his platoon of best friends, he felt useless in the world. And in the end, when all was hopeless, a close friend, who knew and cared for him dearly, helped him out of the mess he had created.

It is extremely important for the survival of our souls to have close relationships. We are blessed with a planet that is full of people to befriend. Do not close you heart and mind to the many people who cross your path. You never know where a good friend may be found.

Bliss Technician Process:

In your journal, make a list of those people who have been supportive of your dreams. Over the next week, write a short thank-you note to each of them. Next, think of ways you can give back, not only to those who've been supportive of your dreams, but to people who need your support. Maybe it's a young person who has the dream of becoming an actor or a handicapped person who would like to participate in sports. It could be an aging parent who needs help with her housework. Sometimes, support simply means calling someone to check in. In any case, there are many people who could benefit from your support. It's important to remember to give as well as to receive.

"The best part of life is when your family becomes your friends and your friends become your family. "

- Danica Whitfield

Chapter 14
Family Matters

Someone once said, "Friends are God's way of apologizing for our families." However humorous this may be, we must strive to have healthy relationships with our families.

Sometimes one of the hardest undertakings is to keep peace and be friends with relatives, immediate or distant. Put the effort into family harmony and communication. Truth is always the best way. There must be open, to-the-point, honest communication within a family—no matter what the subject or situation. Harboring resentment, anger and hostility toward family members will haunt you to the grave. No matter how successful and abundant your life may be, the wounds of family resentment will bind you and keep you from being truly happy.

I realize you cannot make others take action, but you can do what is necessary to get the weight of matters off your shoulders by speaking your truth. If you speak what is on your mind with care and respect for others' views and opinions, you can lift your personal burden and move toward healing the wounds of family pain. Ask only to be heard and to have others respect your decisions. In return, you will honor and respect the opinions and decisions of others. You may not always be able to ease the minds of others, but peace comes from speaking your truth and respecting the views of others simultaneously.

Children want the approval of their parents. They want to live up to their parents' expectations and, although at times it might not be evident, all parents want their children to have the best and to live happily. It's ingrained in human beings to have and protect children, and when people lose their connection to the bliss of life, that disconnect can override their natural instincts to love and protect. This can sometimes cause dissonance within the family as children mature and find their own identities. Adults know what works for them, based on the socioeconomic situations they have experienced. Parents have carved their way in life and know how they would do things in today's world if they were in their children's shoes. With all good intent, parents try to teach their children. Sometimes the children do not listen. Why?

We all have our own dreams, desires and individual characters. As children mature, they begin to understand what they want and how they want to live. This might not be in conjunction with the teachings of their parents. Parents, out of love and protection, often impose their ideals and life strategies on their children, but the children must find their own way of living life. Sometimes we all forget we are different beings with different visions of what life can be.

Giving advice for knowledge, out of love, is one thing, but imposing ideals for control is not healthy for a parent-child relationship. Rules need to be established for the safety and teachings of children, but care must be taken not to smother a child's spirit or dilute or minimize his or her character and individualism.

Likewise, children must know that parents only impose their teachings out of love and protection. They can be as unsure about life as their children are. Parents know what works for them and they do their best with what they know from what they were taught and through their own experiences. Children should explore the knowledge of their parents in greater depth, for parents have a lot of good advice and many ideas to learn from. At the same time, adults should teach and give freely, but try not to mold or control. It is a matter of respect for each other, beyond the parent/child relationship.

Families seem to always fall into the control/rebellion trap. This causes much disharmony within the household. If we are able to see our family as individuals who have much to offer and teach, then we can approach each other with love and mutual respect for each others' values and opinions. We can then create harmony and bliss in the home.

Parents and children must remember that times are so much different today. The world is a dynamic place, and people are as vibrant and ever-shifting as the times. What was ideal in generations past does not always mesh with what's happening today.

Adults and their children must also learn to meet in the middle and compromise. It is important to remember that we do not have to agree with each other's ideas and methods of living life, we just have to respect them. And truly, if no danger or harm comes from unique characteristics, what is the problem? We must discern from living honestly—with truth, integrity and individuality—from living destructively, with unkind behaviors, which are harmful within society.

When we forget mutual respect within family and deny our love for each other, we go awry. Parents resort to restriction and control, while children rebel. Then the parents think their children do not care and do not value their opinions, while children think parents do not care and cannot hear the truth of their being. So they go to separate corners and do not talk to each other. There is no pain deeper than thinking family members do not care for you or see you. This can be changed by listening and mutual respect for others as living human beings.

Jennifer is a very passionate woman. She has a calling of being an intuitive teacher and helping parents and children better communicate with each other. Leaving her well-paying job as a speech audiologist in New Hampshire, Jennifer moved to Boulder, Colorado to further her education and follow her dream. She opened a private practice as an intuitive and spiritual teacher. She is writing a book on the subject and developing a deck of cards to help families communicate with each other.

Jennifer's mother lives in the area and has become her partner in this new business. Bonding together in a new way has been a wonderful and magical experience for both women, after having been separated for many years.

Lately, Jennifer's mother has been suggesting she put her practice on the back burner and become a faculty member at the local university. This would generate money, an insurance program, and give Jennifer the financial grounding she currently does not have. Jennifer is totally against this. From her point of view, her mother is asking her to give up her passions and dreams. But this is not really the case.

Fearful for Jennifer's financial affairs, her mother is trying to impose her ideals out of love and protection. Seeing Jennifer having the education and skills to easily become a member of the university faculty is a way for her mother to fix Jennifer's lacking finances. Jennifer, of course, does not think her mother believes in her and her dreams of becoming a writer and intuitive teacher. They are at an impasse, where only communication, understanding and compassion for each other's visions can see them through to harmony and bliss. It is very important for them to respect and support each other and have frequent talks about their dreams and path for the future. They do not have to agree with the other's opinions and ideas—only have an open mind and respect for the unknown possibilities of what they both have to offer.

What it comes down to is treating others as you would like to be treated. The saying goes, "Do unto others as you would have them do unto you." It does not matter if you are a father, daughter, mother or son, you are a person and your family members are people. They are all individuals, with their own passions, desires and goals for life. Everyone is different with diverse tastes, likes and dislikes. Everyone has something new and unique to offer, if we choose to listen. It makes my heart sing with joy to see family members living together as friends with loving, open communications. These families are living in the flow of bliss, with a joyful harmonious existence.

Problems between parents and children should be resolved immediately, no matter what the situation or the age of the family member. There is no deed unworthy of forgiveness. This does not mean you can forget certain acts. I know some inhuman, harmful and unlawful actions should never be forgotten, but the people themselves can be shown mercy. If for no other reason than to voice how you felt, how you now feel and how your life has been affected by the acts of family members, it should be said. By healing the situation surrounding family actions, you can begin to heal yourself and become more blissful with your life.

A childhood friend of mine, at a young age, was sexually abused by her father. The action never came to light publicly and no legal proceeding occurred. As she grew into adulthood, the trauma of what happened directed her actions and decisions in her life. She drank and occasionally used drugs. She got involved with men who were unhealthy for her and perpetuated more problems. On the rare occurrence when she dated a nice man, she would go out of her way to ruin the relationship by drinking and flirting with other guys. She had a deep-seated hatred for her father and wished him dead.

After years of therapy, she felt she needed to confront her father with what had happened. She mustered the courage to bring into the light what was now an almost 25-year-old wound. She did not forget the act, but she did have the strength to forgive her father. She let him know her feelings and how he had affected her life. From there, she began to rapidly heal herself and become an integrated, loving woman. She met a good man, and now is married with a beautiful child. She even occasionally chats with her father.

If only for the sake of moving toward a more blissful life, you should get your feelings out. If you have unresolved family matters, just your intent of self-healing will make a world of difference in your life. Even if the other party is unwilling to accept or give love and forgiveness, if you release the pain, it will subside for you. You will feel so much better, and it will help you deepen your connection with the bliss of life.

Bliss Technician Process:

Write a heart-felt letter to a friend or family member who you are having or have had problems with. This can be either to someone who is living, or who has passed. Without judgment, voice your feelings regarding the situation. Do not blame or condemn this person, just write how you feel and why this person causes or caused you pain. As you write your views and opinions, remember to be respectful.

After you write your letter, put it down for a day or two and then re-read it. As you read through your letter, make sure it voices your concerns and feelings without blaming, condemning or being hateful to the receiver. When you are satisfied with what you have written, send it to the person. If the person has passed, you can bring it to their grave, read it out loud, leave it or bury it, if allowed. If visiting the grave is not an option, you can read it aloud, then burn it, toss it in the ocean, or bury it. The spirit world is alive and will hear.

Do not expect a reply. Just know you have been heard and you have released the burden of pain from your shoulders. You can never control others' actions or emotions. That is up to them. If they desire to heal, you may hear from them. Feel good about yourself and honor yourself for having the courage to speak out and free yourself from this pain.

"Life without love is like a tree
without blossom and fruit."

- Khalil Gibran

Chapter 15
Romantic Endeavors

One of the most worthy pursuits we can embark
on is the quest for true love. I don't mean just
temptation or a companion on a dark, cold night, but a
true soul mate who is perfectly complementary.

To know true love is to first understand
ourselves. If we are hiding in the shadows, unable or
unwilling to let our true selves shine through, we will be
unable to recognize a soul connection when it happens.
When we have a pessimistic mind-set and are frustrated
with our lives, it is hard enough to love ourselves, never
mind another. To experience love with another, we
must completely accept and understand who we are
inside first. No one and nothing can fill the emptiness in
your soul. When you connect with the bliss of life and
know and accept yourself, love will be within you and
you won't have to look for it anywhere. It is then, when
you least expect it, the miracle will occur.

Some years back, while I was in music school, I
knew a couple who seemed perfect for each other.
When talking with either of them, they both professed
their love and knowing of each other's role in their lives.
Anyone who saw them together commented on how
good they looked together and how lucky they were to
have found their soul mates so early in life.

The first six months of their relationship was
like heaven. They complemented each other in so many

ways and were very involved with each other's lives. At about seven months into the relationship, there was a discussion about the future and marriage.

After this point, they started having problems. Then she disappeared. He was devastated, and longed to reconnect with his true love. His efforts were thwarted no matter how hard he tried. Several months later, she resurfaced as though nothing had happened. When he questioned her about what had happened and where she had been, she said it didn't matter, because she was now back. He was so glad to have her back that he reluctantly accepted her answer.

A few months later, she disappeared again—this time, for almost a year. Yet when she came knocking on his door again, he happily let her in. He felt strongly that they were meant for each other and everyone else agreed. They were getting along well and planning to spend their lives together when she vanished yet again.

A few years passed before she resurfaced. When she returned this time, she professed her undying love for him. She confessed she was insecure about herself and she did not believe she was worthy of such a loving relationship. She said she had thought of him every day. She said she could not go on anymore without at least telling him how she felt.

As nice as her remarks were, they were not enough to mend the heartaches of the past. He could not see through the pain she had caused him. Neither of them had the strength and inner knowing to keep the relationship strong and healthy.

Everyone wants to be in love and have companionship. It seems ingrained in us to search for such a relationship. But mostly I find that people are willing to settle for less than they truly desire. Subconsciously, we are always seeking a more loving, blissful life. When our minds are focused on the negative, we externalize our search for completion. This, of course, only leads to heartbreaks. As I've said before, no one and nothing can complete you or bring you happiness but yourself.

As I look at my own life, I see similarities in my behaviors. My desire for companionship sometimes outweighed the search for true, soulful love. Often when I knew my time in a relationship was over, I hung on anyway for the pure sake of companionship, not love. We often get comfortable with much less than love, because to break away means being alone again.

I once dated a woman who I had a great relationship with. We got along famously and seemed to complement each other wholly. Seven months into our courtship, I proposed, and she happily accepted. We had such a good time together, exploring the depths of life, love and adventure. We were making plans to settle down and start a family—the whole scenario seemed so perfect. But as time passed, I found my path heading in a different direction. My way of living, my goals, my dreams and my spirituality were quickly changing and evolving. As this happened, I began to re-evaluate our common goals.

I loved her dearly but I found our common ground slipping away and the gap in interests growing quickly. I knew she deeply longed for a family, but my new ventures were taking me further away from that reality. In meditation, I felt the energy of the relationship ending. I felt we had taught each other the lessons we'd both needed and it was time to move on. Although my spirit embraced this change, my ego wanted to hang on and stay in the relationship. As time passed, we both were unhappy. She finally decided to leave. The differences in what we each wanted for our future outweighed our mutual love.

After this, we tried to keep it together for several months, but we knew that the essence of our relationship was over. For three more months, we clung to nothingness. I believe we both wanted to be loved, and going back out on our own was scary and potentially hurtful. I was sad to see her leave, but now we both are free to finally search for the kind of relationships we want.

I have learned to embrace this time alone, to reflect on the time and lessons I've learned. I do believe we are sent romantic partners to teach us how to live and love before our true soul mate will emerge. Both you and your perfect other are on the same path of purity and truth, learning with every situation and relationship. You must take these lessons and reflect and learn from them. Life is a school and everyone who crosses your path has a lesson the teach you. Learn these lessons and cherish the time you spend with the wonderful people the universe sends your way.

I have contemplated my past relationships and have found a pattern. Each person was just what I needed at the time. Each brought to me the one missing ingredient for me to evolve further in my life. Each showed personality traits and characteristics of what I truly am searching for. As I ponder this truth and take all the good qualities from each experience, I draw closer to who I am looking for.

I do not go into each situation looking for a romantic connection—quite the opposite. I seek only the experience of meeting a new, like-minded soul, without expectation. I seek to mold the reality of my twin flame and manifest her into my life. We can only bring to ourselves what we can think of. So if you have less-than-perfect expectations or no idea what you want in life, how can the universe answer you?

It is important to know yourself and what you want. Make a list of attributes and characteristics of the person you are looking for. Outline values, morals, likes and dislikes. The more detailed you get the better off you will be with your search. I have done this with tremendous results.

My last encounter was an incredible learning experience for both of us. While on vacation in Florida, I met an amazing woman. She radiated with light, creativity and power. She was physically beautiful, with an ageless wisdom. I saw an image of perfection, my ideal. In her eyes I saw the depths of the universe and the cosmos welcoming us. We could have hastily started a relationship, which I'm sure would have been wonderfully satisfying, for the time being. But both of us, traveling down very similar spiritual paths, recognized there was something missing. Although the connection was there, we knew the timing was off. We recognized the differences in our current places in life and chose to part as friends. I have such a healthy respect and admiration for her, and we will stay friends.

I know we both learned a tremendous amount from the experience, and we are much more powerful for standing in our truths with integrity. Yes, we are both still alone—physically. But meeting her brought me as close as I have ever been to knowing my soul mate and I thank her for that experience. I also know the universe smiled down upon both of us for making the "right" decision of our own free wills.

For those of you in search of love, search with heart. Embark into the unknown with eagerness and passion. Know what you want and do not be afraid of being alone. Have the strength to recognize a relationship that is good but has simply lost its spark. Look at the best in all relationships, and learn the lessons. Walk proudly, and know that Eden is only a thought away!

Bliss Technician Process:

Know yourself and what you want. If you feel you are with your soul mate, celebrate. Do something special, just the two of you. If, however, you are single, then in your journal, make a list of attributes and characteristics of who and what you are looking for in a relationship. Outline values, morals, likes and dislikes. Think about habits, tastes, and lifestyle. List hobbies, music, background and interests. Outline what you feel is good looking and sexy, and yes, what are looking for sexually. The more detailed you get the better off you will be with your search.

If you are currently in a relationship, make the same list. Evaluate whether you have what you need for a happy, healthy, long-term relationship. If you feel it may be a time for a change—then it probably is.

"Lord, I do not want wealth, nor children, nor learning.
If it be Thy will, I will go to a hundred hells,
but grant me this, that I may love Thee without
the hope of reward, unselfishly love for love's sake."

-Hindu Prayer

Chapter 16
Love

     J. Krisnamurti's definition of love has rung clear in my mind for well over a decade now. He writes: "*Love is to give one's self completely, without asking for anything in return.*" If we truly hold the essence of this definition in our minds, we can see how liberating a love of such unselfishness can be. If we can give, unselfishly, without expectations, then we truly have learned how to love.

     The most natural love I see is between parents and a newborn baby. Think of it, a baby cannot give anything except more dirty diapers! Parents give to their children wholly and unselfishly. Parents receive great joy from just watching a child sleep. They love and protect their babies without asking for anything in return.

     This is an example of true love, but this does not have to be limited to parents and children. We can learn to go forth into loving relationships without expectation of the other. We must learn just to love someone for exactly who they are, and not expect or ask of anything from them. When we put demands on people out of "love," it is not love at all. There is a difference between giving generously out of free will and doing chores due to pressures and feelings of obligation. There is a difference between being grateful and appreciative when people give of themselves to you, and putting demands and restrictions on their lives for your own benefit. This basically categorizes the difference between healthy, mature love and a codependent relationship based on insecurity and neediness.

When I was in college, I dated a woman I thought I loved dearly. Inside, I felt she was my soul mate. I had an unhealthy desire to be near her all the time. She was beautiful, fun and charismatic. I was tremendously attracted to her. After a short while dating her, I began to see things in her I did not like—habits I thought unbecoming, which I had gladly accepted at first. She ate poorly, drank too much soda and smoked. She routinely did not have a job and lived with her parents. This was who she was. However, I began to feel she should be different.

By putting demands and expectations on her that were beyond her ability to accommodate, I ultimately ended our relationship. In retrospect, I believe I did love her, but I wanted her to be someone she was unable to be. I wanted her to morph into what I needed, into my ideal. I never thought of what she wanted or needed, or who she really was—only what she could do for me. So my love was trivial. I needed her to be something she could not be. I held on for the sake of having someone around.

It is not love to expect someone to change to fit your needs and desires. If you cannot accept them 100% for who they are and who they will become, then you can never experience the bliss of true love.

It is said that those who try to transform others are actually seeing things in themselves that they do not like. We seem to seek people who are similar to us, in the hope of helping and understanding ourselves. We feel if we can help them change for the better, then somehow we will be better too. But really, this does not work. It is much more powerful to look in the mirror, seek out who we really are, and go from there. We must be able to accept and love ourselves before we can truly give ourselves and love someone else.

When asked what his day of enlightenment was like, the Buddha replied, "It was the saddest day of my life." Why was this? To truly know and accept ourselves is to know our mistakes and weaknesses. We must see to the core of our own being and dredge up all the negative behaviors and unbecoming patterns, which block us from universal bliss. We do not have to change them all immediately, just know and accept who we truly are, how we behave and react. If we accept who we are, with all our negative and positive aspects, we will begin to love ourselves. "Know thyself" and you will open the floodgates to the constant stream of love, harmony and connection to the bliss of life.

Through meditation, you can begin to have a dialogue with yourself and get to know the essence of who you are. You will begin to unlock what you desire; you will know your strengths, weaknesses and fears. You will see the entire you as others see you. You will be more humble and accepting of those around you. When you begin to accept and love yourself for who you are, you will be able to give of yourself wholly, in blissful love.

If you've ever seen two people who know themselves and are together in love, you know how it can inspire you to try to attain the same kind of harmony and togetherness they have created with each other. I have had the opportunity to be in the presence of such a couple.

Steven Farmer and Doreen Virtue share an amazing relationship. They have both been married before and have learned and grown from their experiences. They each spent a lot of time learning about themselves and learning how to love their true essence. When they were finally drawn together, they were able to give themselves to each other with love.

Steven and Doreen are not only married, but work together as writers and speakers. They spend a lot of time together at home and on the road. Those who know them well say they have the most amazing and loving marriage. I have had the opportunity to see them together both at home and professionally and I agree that their relationship is special and powerful.

I have noticed one thing that stands out in their relationship: communication. They talk and share with each other all the time. Communication is a key element in a blissful, loving relationship.

When in a loving, romantic relationship, bliss can be attained by being open, honest and compassionate with each other. Mutual respect must be given and each must honor the other's space. Open communication and sharing thoughts of desires and fears can bring partners to an opulent state of enduring love.

Lovers must remember there are many truths and they will sometimes not agree or understand the paths of the special people in their lives. But this is okay. We are all different, and we must learn to embrace these differences. We do not have to understand or even agree with the choices of others, we just have to love the person and respect what they feel is their truth.

Learning to fully accept and embrace the differences in each other and lovingly honoring and respecting your partner's truth will bring your relationship to a new level of intimacy. Communication is one of the most important fundamentals in keeping an intimate relationship going strong. If you cannot talk to your lover, if you cannot share your hopes and dreams, emotional walls will rise, fears will surface and the relationship will dwindle.

The expression "silence is deadly" is so true in terms of the life of a relationship. When you retreat to a place of silence, your partner does not know what you are thinking or doing. He or she will imagine all sorts of scenarios, which mostly are anything but the truth. Think of a time, at home or work, when you thought the worst was happening, only to find out it was just a the story in your mind. Because others were not openly communicating, you created dismal fantasies about what you thought was going to happen or happening. Only when you found out it was a surprise birthday party for you did you feel foolish—yet set free. When you know what is going on, you can choose your reaction out of knowledge and not speculation.

I once met a woman who captured my heart and soul. After we had been dating a while, I had thoughts of marriage, but I was scared. Our relationship was going very well and we spent all our free time together. My family loved her as much as I did and everyone was very happy and optimistic about our future together. As spring approached, I found myself shopping for rings, but I told no one. I never divulged my feeling of wanting to spend my life with her to her or anyone else. I was petrified of commitment.

She subtly brought up the discussion of the future many times, but always I parried her advances and changed the subject. It did not take long for her to think I was not interested. The summer was winding down, the September winds were blowing and she was getting uneasy with our relationship. I, on the other hand, was getting comfortable with the fact that she was true and would not hurt me or try to force me to change my ways. I made up my mind that if things were going well after a year, I was going to propose at Thanksgiving. I still never let on how I felt and she reached her breaking point.

One day while I was at work, she came to see me. She had one intent: to get some kind of commitment from me. Not a proposal, but a simple "I love you and I'm thinking of a future together." As she cornered me in the showroom of my business, all my fears surfaced. I could not bring myself to let her know how I felt and what I was thinking. Crying, she walked out the door, vowing never to see or talk to me again. She is a woman of her word and I have never seen her again.

If I had simply let her know I had been thinking of a future with her, she would have left the store happy, and things may have been different. I do wish I'd had the strength and courage to tell her how I felt. She had a powerful influence on my life and she made me happy. I still sometimes wonder what my life would be like now if I had only told her I loved her.

There is a lot to learn on the subject of love, and I encourage you to read and understand as much about love as possible. Delve into the study of yourself to uncover your true essence. Remember the words of motivational and spiritual teacher, Sonia Choquette: "You are not good. You are not bad. You are divine." Know yourself. Love yourself. Be open and honest with the ones you love and you will know bliss first hand.

Bliss Technician Process:

In your journal write a love letter to your romantic partner. Tell him or her how you feel, and do not hold back. Let them know how happy they make you and how glad you are that they are in your life. Write a few examples of the little things they do that make you smile. Now go buy a blank card, and transpose you letter to them inside of it. Now give it to them. It will make a big difference in your relationship.

If you are not in a relationship, then write a heart-felt thank you note to someone who has helped or impacted you positively.

"Spontaneity is the quality of being able to do something just because you feel like it at the moment, of trusting your instincts, of taking yourself by surprise and snatching from the clutches of your well-organized routine, a bit of unscheduled plea."

- Anonymous

Chapter 17
Being Flexible and Spontaneous

Those who are rigid and set in their ways bring themselves so much unwarranted emotional stress. By being unwilling or unable to adapt to the ever-changing circumstances of the world around them, they sometimes develop a fear of change and uncertainty. Since the world is always changing and our futures are uncertain, this causes many people tremendous problems in coping with everyday life.

In Eastern Zen philosophies, a lot has been written about the importance of being flexible. Flexibility is a sign of the vibrant and healthy, whereas sternness is rigid and old. Zen masters often use an analogy of a tree when speaking of flexibility. The supple, bendable tree can withstand the storm of the century, while the stern, un-giving trees easily break and fall under the pressures of the gales. We can choose to fight the winds of change and uncertainty with sternness and rigidity, or we can adapt and go with the flow. There is no bliss in doing battle with the inevitable. However, harmony can be found with adaptation and flow.

My good friends Dave and Michelle wanted to move into a new home. They had grown unhappy with the shared driveway and the proximity to their neighbor's house. Their yard was small and they wanted a bigger area for their three children and Dave's workshop and garage. They decided to sell their home and move the family to a nice country house with extra land. Dave was determined to move by late fall, but problems with selling and finding the right home kept creeping up. The more dead ends Dave ran into, the sterner he was about moving. Deals to purchase his home fell through and homes he was interested in either sold quickly to others or were out of his price range.

As the holidays approached, Dave and Michelle decided they would have to stay for a few more years, to better prepare for such a huge undertaking. They had three young daughters and were working full-time, so slowing down and considering all the options seemed like a good thing to do. It was obvious they were not moving to a new home any time soon.

Dave took some time off from thinking about the situation. He decided if he could not move, he perhaps could make his current home more enjoyable for the family, so he set out to remodel. One day, Dave struck up a conversation with his neighbor, whose home had been for sale for quite some time. He asked if they were having any luck selling their home, and was told no.

That night Dave had an idea. He and Michelle talked about the option of simply buying the home next door and turning it into two rental apartments. This would take care of all his problems, plus add the benefit of extra income. He could re-do the driveway and claim the backyard as his own. The garage on his neighbor's property would be his new storage unit and his current garage would be the workshop. They could split the home into two apartments and have a nice income stream. Dave and Michelle made an offer on the home and soon they were remodeling it for tenants. Long before Dave completed the work on the apartments, there was a waiting list to move in.

Dave's steadfastness about buying a new, expensive home had blocked him from seeing other viable options—right under his nose. When he slowed down, relaxed and became more flexible about his situation, miraculous things happened. The answer to all his problems was hidden within the very place he longed to get away from.

Ironically, when we connect with the bliss of life, our problems sometimes become the solutions. We must learn to flow effortlessly, like the waters of a stream. Water does not confront obstacles with force, but gently encompasses and rolls around all barriers. Sometimes it has to veer from the straight path, however it always effortlessly finds the ocean it sets out to join. There are many solutions to the problems in our lives and there are as many different paths that result from the solving of these problems. When we are able to be flexible and flow with the natural bliss of life, we can easily see new opportunities and change direction without stress.

We have to learn to be more like we were when we were young. As children, we were blessed with a certain enthusiasm for living life. Every day was a new adventure—every endeavor a fun learning experience. We concentrated on the task at hand and not necessarily on the outcome. If something was not working, we were quick to change direction or strategy. As children, we enjoyed and embraced the spontaneity of the day, because we somehow understood that the day was sacred—not tomorrow, not yesterday, but today we had the option to live and have fun. We knew as children that "right now" was in our control and we did not want to waste any time having problems, so we went with the flow. We were flexible and entertained our whims for the sake of truly living and enjoying the adventure of life. Learn from children. They have not yet disconnected themselves from the bliss of life.

Being spontaneous is a very important aspect of living a blissful life. Freedom is important to us and we often feel like slaves to the clock and to the circumstances in our lives. I have found that by exercising spontaneity, not only can we realize bliss, but we can also embrace freedom.

Acting from your heart and doing something you truly desire on a whim is a powerful way of taking control of your time and the situations of life. Exercising spontaneity is empowering and infuses you with the knowledge that you are in control of your time and space. When we fall prey to our routines and the demands of the clock, we lose our sense of control and freedom. No harmony or joy comes from living shackled to the hands of a clock.

Being spontaneous does not mean neglecting your professional and personal responsibilities, it's more the habit of loosely scheduling the in-between times of your day and the time you have control over. Following the voice of your spirit, those subtle inner desires, can lead you to amazing places and people. Living more naturally and spur-of-the-moment and not so structured in routines and habits will allow you to live more connected to the flow of bliss and feel more in control of your situations and destiny.

Wendy was a middle-aged factory worker with almost enough time logged to retire. She was at the same job since her early twenties and was unhappy and depressed with the structure and circumstances of her life. An avid cigarette smoker with a poor diet, Wendy was unhealthy and very out of shape. She knew it was time for a change, but for years kept living by the routines she had created for herself. One day while running errands, she stopped by my scuba diving store. On a whim and totally out of character, she expressed interest in learning to dive, despite the fact that she could not swim very well and was petrified of the water.

Wendy had some major obstacles to overcome during her scuba diving course. The first night of class she was so nervous, she had to jump out of the pool, run to the ladies' room and throw up. She stuck with it and after several months of extra practice, she earned her certification. This led Wendy down a new road of bliss. She fell in love with diving. The power of accomplishment propelled her to continue her aquatic education and several years later, she became an instructor. She quit her factory job and moved south to work in a dive shop full time. Last I heard, she was happily teaching scuba diving and living a much happier life.

Wendy stepped out of her routine when she stopped by Fathom Divers that day. Through her courage and ability to take control of her time and space, she found a life-changing avenue of joy.

Being spontaneous means having the ability to be more flexible with your time and space. Rigidity always leads to conflict, and disconnects us from the bliss of life. Flexibility does not mean blindly going with the flow and following others, rather forging new situations by being open to adaptation. There are so many unknowns in life. By being flexible and willing to try new things and travel new roads, you can bring yourself more joy and excitement.

Keep the saying "Okay, I'll try that," at the forefront of your mind. It is the willingness to try and experience new ways of doing things. Experience what is out in the world first hand. Incorporate what you like and what works for you into your life. This is the way to stay flexible. You will not like everything you try, but you will know what is in your core. By being open to the suggestions of others, we can see what and who we truly are through the unknown of what we are willing to try.

Practice flexibility. Make it a habit in your life. If you are very structured and rigid, be open to the idea there may be a better or different way that will bring you more joy and peace. Do more listening to those around you and experiment with others' ideas and ways of doing things. You will find balance, harmony and bliss through being flexible and researching new ideas and concepts.

Bliss Technician Process:

In your journal, write about something you find intriguing. This week, find out more about it. If you can, talk with someone who does it or has done it in the past. When you are comfortable, try it out for yourself.

Take a walk or a drive. Don't plan it; just go. Let your instincts guide you. Go down an unfamiliar road or trail, or travel to a town, shopping area, or neighborhood you have not been before. Stop when you feel the need, or when something interests you. Boldly go—you never know what mystery and adventure awaits you.

"He who lives in harmony with himself lives in harmony with the world."

- Marcus Aurelius

Chapter 18
Meditation

There is nothing more powerful than meditation to connect you with the flowing bliss of life. Meditation often has a confusing stigma because of its religious and metaphysical overtones.

In Eastern cultures, meditation is used to train the mind to be empty or calm. This can be done by focusing on a single object or sound and concentrating on controlled breathing. Western culture tends to define meditation as contemplative thinking or reflection, especially in a deliberate and calm manner.

Meditation is simply relaxing and thinking. However it is directed, deliberate thinking about what we intend. If we can direct our thoughts to what we want to bring into our lives, we will subconsciously make decisions in our daily lives to move closer to those outcomes. When we meditate on peace, love, harmony and joy, we bring the bliss of life into our hearts and minds. Through quiet contemplation, we can begin to understand the implications of how we live our lives and the steps we can take to make the world a better place.

There are many ways to meditate. I suggest finding a way that resonates with you personally. Remember, meditation is a form of directed quiet contemplation. Where can you go to be quiet and think? I have found many outlets for my meditative desires, from traditionally posturing myself and breathing to long walks at night to a Sunday drive alone through the wooded and mountainous areas of my state. I have biked, swum, listened to instrumental music, and just lain on the hammock in my back yard, looking up at the passing clouds. With practice and intent, you will be able to meditate just about anyplace, bringing into your heart and mind that quiet bliss we so long to have.

Recently on a trip to California, my return flight situation was more than stressful. It happened to be a holiday and there were a lot of people flying. The weather was bad across the country, causing many delays, and the airline's computer system was down. People could not get confirmed on the flight and most of us did not have seat assignments. The attendants at the gate were hand writing boarding passes and selecting seats for travelers by hunting and picking. Tensions were rising and many people were conspicuously frustrated and angry. The flight, of course, was running forty-five minutes late, to top it all off.

I found myself getting caught up in the energy of the moment. I was getting antsy, frustrated and impatient. I went up to the podium to ask when I could get my seat and was told I would be called when they got to it.

The attendant was very stressed and visibly angry. She looked at me and said, "Sir, we're doing all we can. Please have a seat."

I took a deep breath and retreated to a chair with a view of the Santa Ana Mountains. As I looked toward the peaks of the range, I noticed the swiftly moving clouds and how beautiful they looked silhouetted by the mountains. I realized the plane would take flight, whether I was stressed or not, so I melted into a meditative state, envisioning getting home safely and on time. I must have sat staring out toward the Santa Anas for about forty minutes when I finally heard the call for boarding. Instead of fighting the mad rush for boarding, I chose to just sit and let everyone else fight their way down the isle. I continued to sit in quiet contemplation until I heard the final boarding call for my flight. I calmly walked onto the plane and took my seat. I put my head back and continued to meditate. Soon I was home.

It's funny, the plane took off and I got home right on schedule without a hitch. I was in a good mood and stress-free; I felt great, in fact. I thought about all those people at the originating airport who were uptight and angry about the uncontrollable situation they were in. They allowed the circumstances to dictate their emotions. This negative energy was contagious, and overtook most all of the passengers and crew alike. Their frustration and anger had no effect on whether the plane could take off on time. Similarly, my calm, meditative state also had no effect on the day's outcome, except I felt good and happy all day. I chose to direct my mind to more pleasant thoughts and take control of what I actually had power over—my state of mind. Calmness and bliss can be achieved any time, any place through meditation by actively directing our thoughts and state of mind to a place of harmony, joy and peace.

Those who practice meditation regularly get pleasantly addicted to the blissful mind/body connection that can be achieved. Millions of people from across the planet realize the transformational powers of routine meditation. Most people I know schedule it into their day. In several cultures, lifestyles actually revolve around the spiritual essence of quiet contemplation.

It is widely believed that self-realization and God-realization can be attained through strict meditative practice. Many claim that, through certain meditations, contact with the spirit world is possible. Some have even boasted to be able to see the past and future. No matter what your belief regarding the possibilities for meditation may be, it is undoubtedly a powerful tool that can help center you in a place of bliss.

"Can I mediate?" I am often asked. To answer this question, I'll ask you only two simple questions: 1. Can you breathe? 2. Do you have a mind? If you answered yes to both of these questions, you can meditate.

There are, of course, thousands of variations of meditation. Your local bookstore or library is stocked with books on the techniques of the many ways to meditate and achieve enlightenment. I focus on the simple technique of relaxing, breathing and directing my thoughts to achieve a more centered, blissful state of being.

Even for the busiest person, there is always time to meditate, if only for a few moments several times during the day. Even short power-meditations will help bring calmness to you.

1. *Waking Meditation*: Upon waking in the morning, before you get out of bed, spend five minutes in quiet thought.

2. *Shower Meditation*: If your morning shower is a quiet time for you, this is a great place and time to think about your day and set your intention to be actively blissful.

3. *Cooking/Cleaning*: Some of my friends who love to cook and clean claim it to be meditative for them. It doesn't work for me, but perhaps you too can use this time to connect.

4. *Driving*: Try to actively keep a smile on your face and take in all the beauty of the natural surroundings. Do not get yourself caught up with others' poor driving manners. Keep focused on peaceful thoughts. Driving can be harder to do in traffic or in cities, but generally this approach is effective in rural areas and

country roads. Caution is warranted here. Do not to get too deeply into a meditative state while driving. Please do not listen to guided meditation CDs in the car.

5. *Lunch Breaks*: Instead of going out with the gang from work for lunch, find a quiet place where you can eat alone in peace. Use this time for a mini-power meditation.

6. *Walking/Hiking*: Walking or hiking is one of the most powerful meditative activities that you can do. Go alone or with a friend who has similar intent. This can be amazingly transformational. The power of being outside and in Nature cannot be diminished and is a perfect place to achieve a deep, pensive mind-set.

7. *Health Club*: Even if your health club is full of chatty or grunting exercise enthusiasts, you can still achieve a meditative state while working out. Treadmills, rowing machines and climbers offer a great way to escape, if only for a short time.

8. *Swimming/treading water*: Usually, no one can bother you and you cannot hear other people while swimming. Because of the constant and routine body movements, entering a meditative state often comes quite easily for those who swim.

These are only a few examples of times and places you can meditate. It is not necessarily the place, but the intent that connects you to the flow of bliss. Besides these simple techniques, I would again suggest that you browse your bookstore for books on the subject. There are also many guided mediation audios and videos to enhance your experience. Guided meditation is a powerful way to quickly connect with your higher self and the universal mind. Try many different techniques to see which one works best for you.

Bliss Technician Process:

First, find a quiet place where you will not be disturbed. Schedule ten to fifteen minutes for your meditation. As you achieve deeper states, meditate as long as you have time. I personally schedule at least thirty minutes a day, with at least once a week at an hour or longer. Put on a CD of easy listening instrumental music of your liking. (I use classical or more melodic musicians who play guitar, piano or different variations of the flute.) Keep this playing softly in the background. You may even choose not to have music and instead use CDs of nature sounds and the outdoors.

Sit or lie comfortably. Breathe rhythmically and slowly in through your nose and out through your mouth. Imagine a beautiful, tranquil place, where there is perfect harmony and peace. Imagine walking through this place. Everyone you meet is happy and completely connected with the bliss of life. Think of yourself being enveloped by an atmosphere of harmony and co-habitation, where everyone has genuine concern for the well-being of others. Think of how you would be and how you would act if you too were motivated by only love for one another, if harmony in family, community and workplace were your goals, if your mission were to create win-win situations out of all disputes, while remaining calm, centered and rational amid conflict.

As your time in contemplation comes to an end, keep this feeling in your heart and mind, and seek to keep the essence of what you imagined with you all day. When you are able to do this, you will find your old behavior patterns slowly giving way to actions of empowerment and support for those around you. You will look at everyone as divine children of Heaven, and realize we are all capable of knowing this blissful place. Through your actions of living in the flow of bliss, others will find their way. If you only make a difference in the life of one person, you will have made the world a better place.

"We are never more discontented with others than when we are discontented with ourselves."

- Henri Frederi Arnier

Chapter 19
Take care of yourself

The importance of self-care is overlooked by many. People often forsake their personal needs in order to please everyone around them. They forget the link between looking good and feeling good. Where is the logic in having a clean home, a spotless car, a perfectly organized desk and a manicured lawn, if you are unhealthy, un-groomed and out of shape?

It seems odd to me that your health—the most important possession you have—is often the one most neglected. What is the good in striving for anything if you won't be around to enjoy it? So much stress and self-loathing comes from being unhealthy and having a poor self-image. Our self-worth is lowered when we look in the mirror to see our muddled, disheveled selves. Without proper diet and exercise and healthy grooming habits, we feel bad. This affects our mental and physical well-being, and can disconnect us from the bliss of life. When our self-image and self-worth are impaired, we lose the connection to feeling good about ourselves. When this happens, we find it hard to project loving, blissful thoughts toward the world around us. We fall into a negative demeanor, which becomes normal after a while. When we feel poorly about ourselves, we project and react to the world around us with insecurity and fear. We become vengeful, yet unaware of our hurting manner toward others. I see this behavior in many of my peers and also in myself.

Throughout my life, I have been very active and in good shape. Since childhood, I skied, hiked, played tennis and enjoyed many other outdoor sports. I also studied the martial arts, which kept my mind-body connection strong. Of course, when I was a Navy SEAL, I was in very good shape. That training and fitness mind-set carried me into my early thirties.

At 35, however, I went through a very tough time in my life. I was unhappy with the choices I had made. I was discontent with almost everything about my life—my business, where I lived, my relationship. Becoming a single parent only added to the stress and dissonance in my life. Although I loved and still deeply love my son, I was depressed and unhappy.

Within a period of two years, I gained about 70 pounds. I stopped working out and was drowning my depression with copious amounts of food. To make matters worse, I became abrupt and rash with many people who crossed my path. I took my depression out on my family, friends, customers and business associates. Growing more reclusive, I hid in my home, eating away my pain.

Since I had always been in very good shape, being overweight was mentally taxing. I could not accept myself let alone love myself anymore. When I left my house, I looked sloppy. I rarely shaved or combed my hair. Although deep inside I was still the same, my mind only focused on the shell, which I thought to be fat and ugly. I was anything but connected to the bliss of life—I was miserable. My mind could only focus on my external body, which I had created out of choice, but which I loathed.

So many people suffer from the same perpetuating cycle. They are overweight and unhappy with themselves, so they eat more to satiate their needs for fulfillment. Oddly enough, food is used to calm and quiet the body and mind. When we are full, we actually feel fulfilled. You can see how the cycle is never-ending.

When we see ourselves as overweight and we are unhappy and needy, we eat more because it makes us temporarily happy and fulfilled. We feel out of control with our lives, but we can control our food intake. We fill the emptiness with an abundance of food. It's as simple as that. So we become overweight and stay there.

Of course, we are externalizing our problems, instead of seeking answers from within. I was finally reminded that I was not the look and shape of my body, the color of my hair or the clothes I wore. I can never be completely defined by weight, size or proportion. Yes, my body may fit into a certain category, but my spirit, my soul, and my mind cannot be defined by outer appearance. You cannot judge me or anyone else by looks alone.

When I reconnected with the bliss of life, through introspection and meditation, I realized who I was—and it was not some fat guy! I became very comfortable with myself and began to love myself again. When I was able to see things clearly, the doors of peace and harmony opened up for me.

I began to accept myself, wholly and as I was. I became more dapper in dress and groomed in appearance. I started getting compliments on how good I looked. A friend said I had recaptured my inner glow, which I had lost for a few years.

As I began to feel better about myself, dressing better, grooming myself and getting outside and living my life again, the weight began to drop off. Within a short time, I lost over 20 pounds without diet or exercise. As I focused on who I really was inside and not out, my outer body began to again mirror my inner, healthy spirit.

Soon I was even more joyful and happy when I had to purchase smaller pants and a few belts to hold them up! That gave me the motivation to start working out and controlling my diet. I finally went skiing again with some friends, after not participating in the sport for four years. I was elated to be back on the slopes, exercising my body, as the cool wind blew through my hair. As I reconnected with myself, I found myself wanting to do the things I used to love to do.

The body can be changed easily, but knowing and loving yourself is essential to healthy and blissful living. No matter what your physical appearance may be, if you are secure and confident with yourself, it will show. Charismatic people draw people to them not because of what they look like, but because of who and how they are. Look at Oprah Winfrey, for example. She has built one of the most successful daytime television shows in history, and it has nothing to do with her appearance. Through her belief in her abilities, she is successful. Throughout her career Oprah has always dressed well and carried herself fabulously, even though her weight fluctuated drastically over the years.

It is not how you look, but how you feel about yourself that counts. When you feel good about yourself, you tend to be healthier and take better care of yourself. The choice to live a healthier life is yours, as is the choice to connect with the bliss of life.

Overeating is only one way that the lack of love within us can manifest. There are many self-destructive habits that we use for comfort. Almost all of these are due to false perceptions of ourselves. We must change these perceptions to be more accurately in tune with who we really are—divine. With this knowledge we can direct our lives actively toward what makes us happy.

There are those who believe our lives are written. We will die when we die and nothing is going to change that. I don't agree wholly with that philosophy. I think our fate is partly in our hands.

I always like to remind people of the biblical references to "free will." Yes, we have a certain destiny and purpose in life, according to religious texts, but we also have the choice whether to seek and follow our life path. Simply enough, if we choose to live unhealthy lives, partaking of sinful habits, we are choosing to exercise our free wills.

In the movie *Constantine*, Keanu Reeves plays an exorcist who is dying of lung cancer. When asked for the reasons for Constantine's impending death, the Archangel Gabriel answered that he was going to die young because he had smoked cigarettes since he was a kid. Simple as that: he had chosen to smoke, so he would suffer the consequences of his actions.

We are all in charge of our free will to choose our daily routines of health. You do have a choice—an apple over a cookie, juice over a soda, water instead of alcohol, a turkey sandwich in lieu of pizza. You have the choice—a walk around the block instead of watching TV, getting outside on the weekends instead of locking yourself in the house. It's all choice. Choose to live in harmony with the universe and connect with the bliss of life. You will feel—and look—amazing, if you so choose.

Bliss Technician Process:

Do you consider yourself loving, kind, compassionate? Are you helpful? Smart? Creative? Athletic? Write about some of the things that make you special. Ask your family and friends to describe some of your good qualities and what makes you so special in their lives. Now ask yourself this question: "Does my outer appearance dictate these qualities? If you were bigger or smaller, would these qualities still be there?" Does your perception about yourself change the fact that you're a good person? You are not your waist size or the pimple on your forehead. You are not the clothes that you wear or the car that you drive. What makes you special is not the fact that you are 4'3" or 6'11", black, tan or gold. The essence of you comes from within, from the qualities that you have, and not your appearance. List these qualities in length and in detail.

"If you're going through hell, keep going."

-Winston Churchill

Chapter 20
It's not going to be easy

Although walking the path of bliss can be very gratifying and life changing, it is not an easy road. Everyday, you will be tested. Everyday you will doubt your faith. Faith is the key: faith in yourself and faith in your decisions to change your life for the better. When you find yourself against the ropes, when bliss has escaped your grasp and anger, fear and doubt encompass you, take a few moments to calm and center yourself. Give yourself a "time-out." As we give children time-outs to think about their choices and actions, we must do the same for ourselves. Change is very difficult, and sometimes discipline is warranted to re-center and remember our commitment to connecting with the bliss of life.

I am just a man, and I am far from perfect. I do the best I can and strive to grow each and every day. I am committed to bettering my life and myself but sometimes I find myself anything but blissful.

After a car accident, I developed back pain. A year and a half later, my problem persisted and my doctor said I would have to learn to live with the pain. Although routine deep-tissue massages, yoga and lot of stretching did help a bit, my back pain continued. Some days I would feel good, but sometimes my back would bother me for week at a time.

After approximately two weeks of constant, nagging pain, my back just gave out. The pain medications and the Motrin only offered a brief reprieve. I had not slept through a night in over a week, and the constant pain and sleeplessness crept up on me.

My 4-year-old son and I had a very busy June day. The sun was shining brightly, and the temperature was almost eighty. We cleaned the house, cut the grass, washed the truck and did laundry. After lunch we went hiking then ran errands. After dinner, we were both beat. My son fell asleep on the couch, so I carried him off to bed, something I dearly love to do, and decided I would retire also. I was worn out from the day's activities and hoped I would finally get some rest. I was mistaken.

My back throbbed and ached, and sleep was something of a dream. I tossed and turned for hours. I tried sleeping on the floor, the couch and even the spare bedroom. All my efforts were in vain. As sun was starting to light the morning sky, I was very uncomfortable and irritable. I finally dozed around 5:30 a.m.

I was abruptly awakened at 6:05 a.m., when my son decided he wanted chocolate milk. I asked him to please go back to sleep or to play quietly in his room for a while. He refused to honor my request and started to repeatedly scream "chocolate milk" over and over again. I yelled for him to please stop and be quite, but he defiantly continued. I was fuming at that point. I jumped out of bed and stomped my way to his bedroom. As I entered, I stubbed my toe on the rocking chair, sending it flying across the room. "Why can't you please just be quiet?" I yelled. My son cowered under his sheets. I rarely, if ever, yell at him. The relocation of the rocking chair and the hollering really scared him, and he started to cry. I made my way back into my room and plopped back in bed.

His sobbing cut through my head like nails, and I was getting even more angered. I was ready to go back into his room and give him another yelling, but I caught myself. I put myself in a time-out. I was acting poorly, and I needed time to think about my actions. I closed my eyes and covered my head with a pillow. As I started to take a few deep meditative breaths, I remembered something I had read in Marianne Williamson's book <u>The Gift of Change</u>. She said that no matter what is happening to you or in your life, give love to the situation and it will be healed. I had to laugh at myself. I remembered I am not by back pain or my sleepless nights. My body may be worn down, but I still have control over my mind and my choices of how to act. Yes I was exhausted and in pain, but at that moment I chose to not let it control my emotions.

I got out of bed and went to get my son his morning drink of chocolate soymilk. I entered his room with the cup, and a huge smile came upon his little face. I felt great inside, despite my physical condition. "Thank you, Daddy," he said. I asked if he would like to watch his TV for a while, so I could get some more sleep. He, of course, said yes. I gave his small head a rub and started to leave the room. He looked at me and said, "I love you, daddy." "I love you too, buddy," I said as I left his room.

Controlling your behavior in these types of situations can be very tough. It is in the most difficult of situations that we can learn and grow the most. Although I was definitely not very happy or blissful that morning, I did know how to act properly. I thank God for giving me the strength to make the right choices, and I know He is happy with my faith and my commitment to taking the high road. Life is all about challenge and choice. It is not easy, but having faith in yourself and making the correct decisions will make your life so much more blissful. Whether at home or work, you can choose to have a good day and be a blissful example for others.

It goes beyond the question of whether you are doing what you want or like, or whether you are feeling good or bad on a particular day. It goes into your character and how you present yourself to the world. I do not want to set an example for my child, family or friends—the ones who look up to me—that it is okay to compromise my values and integrity just because I am having a bad day or I am doing something I do not want to do. This will cause more stress in life than just doing the task happily. It is a matter of honor and integrity and living in your truth. You can be happy doing an unexciting, tedious task or job. You can have power and bliss in knowing that you choose to live with integrity and honor, no matter what the duty may be. You must realize that all jobs, whether electrician, politician or parent, are a form of service and you are helping someone somewhere, somehow.

There is peace in knowing that you do something that fulfills a need and helps people, even if you do not see the immediate outcome. Look into what you do and find what service provide to others. Do your task. Live your life with honor and truth. Choose to access the bliss of life no matter what you do or how you feel. Do this and you will truly deepen your connection with the bliss of life.

Bliss Technician Process:
Don't Get Discouraged

Do not get discouraged if you cannot connect with the bliss of life overnight. It takes practice and commitment. In jour journal, write your commitment to yourself to follow the path to bliss. Keep track of your accomplishments and your setbacks. Write about what you have learned and how you have grown. Remember the only real tragedy in life is to not learn and grow from ALL of life's experiences, good and bad.

"Peace and friendship with all mankind is our wisest policy, and I wish we may be permitted to pursue it."

-Thomas Jefferson

Chapter 21
The way life should be

Can you imagine a peaceful, blissful existence where all mankind lives in harmony and joy? This is a vision that many people on this earth share. Can you just imagine the possibilities of everyone working together for a common goal of good instead of competing and fighting over the senseless material possessions we give so much value to? Henri Nouwen, an internationally renowned priest, author and respected professor who taught at Notre Dame, Harvard and Yale says, "Much violence is based on the illusion that life is a property to be defended and not to be shared."

If we can cease fighting over the bountiful resources of the earth and unselfishly share with gratitude and love, we can exist without struggle, strife and confrontation. Lyndon Johnson told us that the thousand-mile journey of peace should be taken one step at a time. We must strive—everyday and every moment—to live connected to the bliss of life and project it toward all who cross our paths. We must unselfishly give of ourselves, our resources and our time. The love you send out will return to you tenfold, perpetuating an endless cycle of harmony and bliss for you. Set an example for everyone you come in contact with.

Think of how good you feel when you do something nice for someone. It is powerful and uplifting when you are able to put a smile on someone's face. I have found much joy in giving of my time to others, which is why I chose this career. Knowing I may be able to affect people for the better and help others find a more joyous, peaceful way of life is so incredibly empowering. Just knowing I have the ability to make someone's life better is the driving force behind my writing and speaking.

Just imagine if you allow yourself to capture the essence of harmony and bliss within you and live a joyous, peaceful life. What do you have to lose? What are you waiting for? The universe has sent out an open invitation for all to come join in harmony.

Jesus said, "The kingdom of heaven is within you." Unity, peace and harmony are the ways of heaven. We can have heaven on earth, through intent and thought. We may not live there, but our earthly existence can be heavenly. When Jesus was born, angels bestowed the blessing, "Peace on earth, good will toward men." We must choose the path of bliss to lead us from our state of dissonance and chaos. We cannot bring harmony to our lives if we live with fear, discrimination or condemnation for anyone. We must realize we are all one and we are all on this earth together—for better or for worse.

According to the Bible, Judgment Day is the day at the end of the world when God judges individuals or the human race as a whole. Written in the Gospels and the Book of Revelation: "On this day the Earth and the sky will be in an uproar, the dead will rise from their graves, and Jesus will return to judge all the living and the dead. In judging their conduct, He will consider the deeds people do to each other, both good and bad, as if they had been done to Him."

A Course in Miracles, published by the Foundation for Inner Peace, has a slightly different view of Judgment Day and the second coming of Christ. The

Course says Judgment Day is about us. It is not a specific day. It is when we finally evaluate what is worthy of our time and attention. It is when we will look at the situations in our lives and decide if they are congruent with the highest standards of moral living. A Course in Miracles says that when we finally choose to accept a thought system based on love, without judgment or fear, we will adapt a Christ Consciousness. This adaptation of a Christ Consciousness by the masses is what the second coming of Christ is all about.

We have the free will to choose how we conduct ourselves here on earth. We have the ability to choose to live with love in harmony and peace with one another. Or we can choose to live in dissonance and disdain. If we choose the path of bliss and live in unity without judgment, then we are destined for a heavenly existence here on earth.

So ask yourself how you want to live. How do you want to be seen and known? How do you want to be judged? When it is time for your death, what do you want people to say about you at your funeral? You have the choice to live how you want. Embrace the bliss of life and know and hold the amazing life that can be yours.

Choose the higher path, the way life should be. It takes two to have an argument. If one chooses to not be involved and sends love, forgiveness and understanding to the other, harmony will reign. Be that person who is passive. Do not compromise your truth or integrity. Choose not to argue. Simple. Disarm aggressors with peace and compromise. Offer solutions and not argument. Invite others to join you, and together find the balance and resolution that works for both. Sometimes, it is just better to walk away and accept what is to come, for if you truly are connected with bliss, you will be happy no matter what.

Life can be inspiring and adventurous, if you choose it to be. You can live boldly, experiencing all the world has to offer. There are millions of places to go, people to meet and activities to participate in. The possibilities of excitement and adventure are all around you everywhere, every day. People will watch you from the sidelines, wishing and hoping they could enjoy the game of life as you do. The world is a heavenly, blissful playground. Have fun. Live life and choose to connect with the ever-flowing bliss that surrounds you daily.

Bliss Technician Process:

Eleanor Roosevelt said, "It isn't enough to talk about peace, one must believe it, one must work for it." In your journal, write about how you will work for peace in your household, workplace and in the world.

"Peace is a daily, a weekly, a monthly process,
gradually changing opinions, slowly eroding old
barriers, quietly building new structures."

- John F. Kennedy

Chapter 22
Walk the blissful path and others will follow

The road to bliss is a process—a process within
you, your community, your state, your country and your
world.   Within each of us is the ability to choose
harmony and peace over dissonance and vengeful, fear-
based reactions to situations in life. If we choose to
follow our hearts and listen to our spirits, we can choose
a better way of thinking and acting. We will have an
impact and lasting effect on others and the world
around us.

So if you want to live a blissful life, you have to
be the embodiment of bliss and all the universal
components that connect you to bliss.   Don't just
externalize what you want. Make it your essence. You
have to become what you seek—*be* the essence of what
you desire. Without fear, just be your amazing self, an
embodiment of the facets of bliss. Let these things be
true for you:

1. Be Forgiveness

You have learned to be in a state of clemency
and kindness for others always. It has become your
nature to automatically forgive without a second
thought. It is now part of your soul, your essence, your
core to act with mercy and pardon for all those who
unknowingly bestow pain and suffering toward you.

You hold dear the words of Jesus, as he hung, crucified upon the cross; "Forgive them Father, for they know not what they do."

You are continually exercising forgiveness in your daily life and are able to receive forgiveness from those you have trespassed against. You walk in the grace of the heavens because you know nothing can be more blissful than to know that God smiles down upon you. You *are* forgiveness and your soul has been forgiven.

2. Be Love

You have opened your heart and mind to the divine possibility that everything vibrates at certain levels. You understand lower vibrations of negativity, anger and fear, and higher vibrations of love and compassion. People can feel the "vibes" in the air and they are contagious. You send vibrations of love and joy from the depths of your heart and soul. You find, in turn, you have an effect on the world around you. You don't just talk about loving the earth and mankind, you feel it in your being. Combating the feelings of fear, anger, vengeance and negativity, you have replaced them with thoughts and actions of kindness and love, and live in harmony and bliss with everyone around you and the world.

3. Be Peace

You have peace in your life because you practice peace, every moment of every day. You do not forget your center and the knowledge that peace is only a state of mind—a choice you make. You are quiet and calm and do not become reactive but are active. Close your eyes and breathe in the calmness of the universe. You have planted the seeds of peace deep within, and bliss blossoms from your soul.

4. Be Beauty

Beauty is much more than skin deep—it radiates from inside our souls. Knowing that, you are not afraid to let your tender, creative self shine through. You are joyful and spread happiness. You forgive and are peaceful. Your true inner beauty is seen. You have learned to be loving and true to yourself. Affectionately, you allow your beautiful self to radiate from the depths of your soul. You truly know the essence of your inner splendor and do not keep it hidden within you, but let it shine through for all to see. Because you connect with your inner beauty, people see you as a beautiful person. You inspire others to allow themselves to be beautiful.

5. Be Powerful

You speak your truth with integrity. Standing in your power means to know yourself and what you are doing at all times. With honesty and truth, you stand for who and what you believe in. You respect and appreciate others' opinions and values. You look for a harmonious solution to every situation. You speak with wisdom, not spite. You stay loyal and true to your values and morals. Without fear, you move forward, generously leading the way for those less courageous than yourself. You radiate love and security, and inspire blissfulness and courage through your actions.

6. Be Patience

You are willing to wait and accept the quiet times between action and results. There is no sense of urgency or rush, for you know that scuttling and hurry only leads to stress and dissonance. There is calmness about you as you quietly go about your busy day. Not lazy at all, you are very productive, but cool and exacting in action. You realize life is meant to be savored and those who speed through miss out on the glories of existence. You live in the moment and savor every second of your gift of life. At the end of a hectic day, you are still full of vigor and zeal, for you have not wasted precious energy on hurry, worry and stress. You are looked up to and many seek your counsel, no matter what your position in work, school, community or family may be. You are patient, calm and peaceful. Your powerful essence draws others to you.

7. Be Abundance

You know the meaning of abundance is not being monetarily rich, but wealthy with bliss. You are filled with love, peace, joy and harmony. You spread your abundance selflessly to all you come in contact with. You are a sage, a prophet and a preacher of love and happiness. You empower and motivate through your shining example the knowledge that we need not be rich to have lavish abundance in our lives.

You are forever grateful for what you have and you constantly show your appreciation and respect for those who help you and to the heavens above. You are a pillar of strength and wisdom and freely share the lessons of life you have learned. You have no expectations of others, but endeavor to experience what everyone and what life has to offer. You walk humbly with an open heart, greeting everyone as brothers and sisters on this journey of life. You are a shining example of how people should live—not perfect, just striving to be better than you were yesterday.

As we endeavor to walk the path of bliss—to act out of spirit for the good of all—we venture out alone. We must have the courage to stand true, to know the potential of blissful living. Courage is not the absence of fear, but the ability to move forward into uncertainty while facing your fears. Just the act of commitment and effort will bring you the power to adapt and change.

Know that you will lose some friends, but gain many more. Know you can light the path but you can never make someone walk the road. Not everyone will understand your commitment to living a better life. Most will not have the courage or the will to change their habits and know themselves for who they are. Stand in your truth with integrity and fortitude. Don't fear what others may think. Seek encouragement, wisdom and praise from inside. Know that by following your heart, you will inspire others to follow their own hearts too. Know that when you connect with the bliss of life, your world will be transformed and truly amazing!

Bliss Technician Process:

Practice random acts of kindness. "Random acts of kindness are those sweet or lovely things we do for no reason except that, momentarily, the best of our humanity has sprung into full bloom. When you spontaneously give a stranger the bouquet of red carnations you had meant to take home to your own dinner table, when you give your lunch to the guitar-playing homeless person who makes music at the corner between your two subway stops, when you anonymously put coins in someone else's parking meter because you see the red "EXPIRED" medallion signaling to the meter maid, you are doing not what life requires of you, but what the best of your human soul invites you to do." (Quote by Dawna Markova excerpted from RANDOM ACTS OF KINDNESS with permission of Conari Press, imprint of Red Wheel/Weiser, York Beach, ME and Boston, MA. To order RANDOM ACTS OF KINDNESS please call 1-800-423-7087)

You are not and will never be perfect, but you have chosen to connect with the bliss of life, and to make yourself and the world a better place. It's time to celebrate your choice and celebrate your life. Today, do something special for yourself. Whatever it may be, make it something that will make you feel good. You deserve it.

The Beginning is now...

"When the power of love outweighs the
love of power the world will know peace."

- Jimi Hendrix

I thank God for blessing me with so many amazing abilities, which enable me to follow my dreams and help so many people at the same time.

This book would not be possible if it weren't for so many supportive people. I would like to take this opportunity to acknowledge and thank all who helped me along my path. I am truly grateful to have so many great people in my life...thank you all!

Special thanks go to the following people:

Elizabeth Foley
(www.divinehealing.us)

Doreen Virtue
(www.angeltherapy.com)

Steven Farmer
(www.stevendfarmer.com)

Lynnette Brown
(www.angelicwonders.com)

Jennifer Crews
(www.intuitiveteachings.com)

Gina Heart

Maundy Mitchell

Janette Tomes

Tom Campbell
(www.adibooks.com)

Would you like to be in one of my books?
Send me your Bliss Story!

Do you have an inspiring story how _Connecting with the Bliss of Life_ affected or changed a situation in your life for the better? If you do, I would love to hear about it.

Email your story to me at **blissstory@daveferruolo.com**, or send it to the below address, and you may find yourself featured on our website or in one of my books!

Send your story via postal mail to:

D. Michael Ferruolo, Enterprises
Attn: Bliss Story
PO Box 6421
Laconia, NH 03246

David Michael Ferruolo

Lectures
Workshops
Book Signings
Speaking Engagements

For more information on Dave's schedule, please visit: www.daveferruolo.com

To schedule an event, please contact:

D. Michael Ferruolo, Enterprises
PO Box 6421
Laconia, NH 03246

(603) 556-4360 Voice
(603) 556-4361 Fax
info@daveferruolo.com

Coming Soon from
Dave Ferruolo

Becoming a Bliss Technician
From blah to Bliss in 30 days

Manifest Your Life
How to Create the Life You Want and Deserve

A Smile Goes a Long Way
A Guide Book For Daily Bliss

www.daveferruolo.com

Suggestions for further reading

Choquette, Sonia. *Trust Your Vibes.* Carlsbad: Hay House, 2005.

Covey, Stephen. *The 7 Habits of Highly Effective People.* New York: Simon & Schuster, 1989.

Dyer, Wayne W. *The Power of Intention.* Carlsbad: Hay House, 2004.

Foundation for Inner Peace. *A Course in Miracles.* New York: Foundation for Inner Peace, 1975.

Farmer, Steven D. *Power Animals.* Carlsbad: Hay House, 2004.

Sacred Ceremony. Carlsbad: Hay House, 2002.

Hemingway, Ernest. *The Old Man and the Sea.* New York: Scribner; Reissue Edition, 1995.

Hicks, Ester; Hicks, Jerry. *Ask and it is Given.* Carlsbad: Hay House, 2004.

Osho. *Courage:* The Joy of Living Dangerously. *New York: St. Martin's, 1999.*

Price, John Randolph. *The Abundance Book.* Carlsbad: Hay House, 2005.

Redfield, James: *The Celestine Prophesy.* New York: Warner, 1997.

Virtue, Doreen: *Angel Medicine*. Carlsbad: Hay House, 2004.

    I'd Change My Life If I Had More Time. Carlsbad: Hay House, 1996.

    Losing Your Pounds of Pain. Carlsbad: Hay House, 2002.

    Messages From Your Angels. Carlsbad: Hay House, 2003.

Yogananda, Paramahansa: *Autobiography of a Yogi*. Los Angeles: Self-Realization Fellowship, 1979.

David Michael Ferruolo

Interested in Scuba Diving?

www.fathomdivers.com